A Bigger Table

A Bigger Table

Building Messy, Authentic,
and Hopeful Spiritual Community

John Pavlovitz

WESTMINSTER
JOHN KNOX PRESS
LOUISVILLE · KENTUCKY

© 2017 John Pavlovitz

First Edition
Published by Westminster John Knox Press
Louisville, Kentucky

17 18 19 20 21 22 23 24 25 26—10 9 8 7 6 5 4 3 2 1

Unless otherwise indicated, Scripture quotations are from the New Revised Standard Version of the Bible, copyright © 1989 by the Division of Christian Education of the National Council of the Churches of Christ in the U.S.A., and are used by permission.

Book design by Drew Stevens
Cover design by Mary Ann Smith

Library of Congress Cataloging-in-Publication Data

Names: Pavlovitz, John, author.
Title: A bigger table : building messy, authentic, and hopeful spiritual
    community / John Pavlovitz.
Description: First Edition. | Louisville, KY : Westminster John Knox Press, 2017.
Identifiers: LCCN 2017013697 (print) | LCCN 2017031110 (ebook) | ISBN
    9781611648256 (ebk.) | ISBN 9780664262679 (pbk. : alk. paper)
Subjects: LCSH: Christianity and culture—United States.
Classification: LCC BR526 (ebook) | LCC BR526 .P39 2017 (print) | DDC
    261—dc23
LC record available at https://lccn.loc.gov/2017013697

PRINTED IN THE UNITED STATES OF AMERICA

♾ The paper used in this publication meets the minimum requirements of the American National Standard for Information Sciences—Permanence of Paper for Printed Library Materials, ANSI Z39.48-1992.

Westminster John Knox Press advocates the responsible use of our natural resources. The text paper of this book is made from 30 percent postconsumer waste.

Most Westminster John Knox Press books are available at special quantity discounts when purchased in bulk by corporations, organizations, and special-interest groups. For more information, please e-mail SpecialSales@wjkbooks.com.

This book is dedicated to Jen, Noah, and Selah, to Mom, Brian, Eric, and Michelle, and to my father, John Pavlovitz, who taught me how to be a dad, and who believed in me before I ever went viral. You're still my hero and I miss you.

Contents

Introduction

A Wednesday Morning in November

Some days you don't welcome the sun. Some days you dread it.

From a distance, it could have been just another Wednesday morning in November, but it wasn't. This one was planet rocking. It was foundation shifting. It was faith shaking. On this particular Wednesday morning in November 2016, so much about my country seemed different. On this morning I couldn't help but wake up and feel as though the table had become decidedly smaller—and that religion had helped make it so. As someone who has spent the last two decades in the trenches as a pastor in the local church trying to craft a more diverse, open, expansive expression of the Christian faith, it was a day of deep grieving and profound sadness. There was a sense that we'd squandered a priceless opportunity, that we'd gone backward, that we'd failed one another. It wasn't just the election results themselves; it was the realization that regardless of those results the damage had already been done, the poison had already been released into the bloodstream. We'd seen too much and learned too much to go back to who we'd been before—and going forward didn't quite seem like an option yet. Grief will freeze you if you let it, and I felt frozen. Many of us did.

And it wasn't merely the reality of the man we'd allowed to ascend to the presidency that brought the mourning, though that would be reason enough for despair for many of us. It was the cruelty we'd witnessed in one another as he'd made his way there, the sickness that the America we love had shown itself afflicted with. It was the suffocating weight of every horrible reality about our nation; all that bigotry and discord and hatred set upon our chests, hampering our breath. But it was much closer than that, too. It was the words we'd heard from family members, the things we'd learned about our neighbors, the social media posts from church friends, the incendiary sermons from our pastors, the arguments we'd had with coworkers. It was the stuff we'd learned about ourselves. On this Wednesday morning in November, we woke as a terribly altered people.

Perhaps more than any period in recent history, the yearlong presidential campaign leading up to this particular Wednesday morning had greatly renovated the landscape of religion in my country. The already deep divides had become cavernous, with Americans driven to opposite poles largely along political party lines. The closer Election Day came, the more incendiary the rhetoric grew, the more combustible conversations became, the more civility evaporated. Yes, this had always been somewhat true of our political process, and sadly the recent history of Christianity in America had increasingly been characterized by a growing schism between Left and Right—but this year everything was different. This year any glossy veneer of our diverse coexistence was stripped away and we saw the terrible ugliness beneath with clarity. In fact this ugliness sadly became valuable political currency—something to purchase power with.

Donald Trump ran unapologetically on a platform of exclusion and division, on fear of the other, on protection from encroaching foreign threat. He spoke of building walls and registering Muslims and beating up protesters. Coded in words about "taking back America" and "making America great again," at its core his message was one of a smaller, whiter, wealthier table. And yet despite the vitriol he dispensed and the divisiveness he generated and the violence his campaign yielded at rallies and in rising hate crimes, Trump was somehow embraced by large numbers of (mainly white, conservative) Christians who looked at the candidate's body of work, littered with vile words and moral failings and unscrupulous business dealings—and deemed it all acceptable. As the race wound into the fall, high-profile preachers began aligning themselves with the GOP candidate, leveraging their pulpits and platforms to champion his cause. Local church leaders became less apprehensive about injecting themselves into the political process and more vocal in their support of him. Otherwise strictly sin-intolerant Christians engaged in all manner of theological gymnastics in order to justify Trump as somehow the *lesser of two evil* options.

And with each pastor's public endorsement and with every social media sanctioning, the disconnect between American Christianity and the Jesus of the Gospels became more noticeable to those of us looking closely and grieving it all. We watched the bigger table being dismantled in real time. People both inside and outside of organized religion saw the uneasy alliance of the Church and the GOP front-runner and strained to make sense of it. In fact, in the wake of the campaign, many people already disheartened and pushed to the periphery of organized religion left for good. Trump's eventual victory was for many in typically marginalized communities merely a ratification of the corrosive things unearthed, a ceremonial crowning of it all. It was irrefutable proof that they are not welcome at the table.

For nearly twenty years I've been working with like-hearted people to craft the kind of loving, redemptive spiritual community that could span all divides and would force no one to find alternatives or fend for themselves, community that transcends all difference. I've always believed such a place was possible, and so with great hope that was the book I set out to write eighteen months ago. The toxic venom of the presidential campaign, the wounds it has inflicted on so many, and the Christian church's unprecedented participation in the process during that time has left me certain that our efforts to build a bigger table are more needed than ever, yet in some ways we are further from that aspiration than we've ever been. And so the questions I asked myself on that particular Wednesday morning are the same ones I ask here: Can the table really be expanded so that everyone has a place? What is the way forward, given the unprecedented divisiveness we're experiencing? How do we transform this nearly paralyzing sense of sadness into something worth pursuing?

Many people are grieving the loss of the America they thought they knew; they are mourning their old picture of home or their image of church. As with all grief, eventually there must be *movement*. When there is profound loss of any kind, the only real path is forward; it is trying to create something meaningful and life affirming in response to what has been taken away. As you move ahead from the moment of trauma, you begin the painful, laborious act of living in direct opposition to your grief. You learn to walk again, even if it is with a limp. It is the same in these days for those of us who feel cheated out of a kinder, more diverse, more decent America than the one it feels like we now have. It is the same for those of us lamenting a religion that seems to have become smaller than ever. Individually and collectively, we will have to be the resistance—offering daily, bold, defiant pushback against all that feels wrong here. This pushback will come as we loudly and unapologetically speak truth where truth is not welcome. It will come as we connect with one another on social media and in faith communities and in our neighborhoods, and as we work together to demand accountability from our elected officials and pastoral leaders. It will come in the small things: in the art we create and the conversations we have and the quiet gestures of compassion that are barely visible. It will come in the way we fully celebrate daily life: having dinner with friends, driving through the countryside, playing in the yard with our children, laughing at a movie we love. It will come as we use the shared resources of our experience and our talents and our numbers to ensure that our children inherit a world worth being here for. It will come as we transform our grief into goodness.

Yes, friend, there has been a great deal to grieve over in recent days, and you will likely find more reason to grieve as you read these words—but there is even more worth fighting for. Wherever you are on your journey and whatever your religious and political convictions, consider this an invitation to enter into the conversation. This book isn't about battling dogmas, it isn't about competing faith traditions, and it isn't about opposing politics. This book is about humanity, about the one flawed family that we belong to and the singular, odd, staggeringly beautiful story we all share. It's about trying to excavate those priceless truths from beneath the layers of far less important things that we've piled on top of them since we've been here. It's about jettisoning everything in and around us that would shrink our tables. I'll tell a bit of my story in the coming pages in the hopes that you'll find some of your own story there, and I'll share the lessons I've acquired through time, failure, scars, mentors, and people much wiser than I. Yes, one day in November did indeed change everything. We need the bigger table now more than ever.

Pull up a chair.

PART ONE

Big God, Small Table

1

Finding My Place

Before I knew better, I assumed that everyone had a seat at the same table that I did. For nearly the first two decades of my life in perpetually snow-blanketed Central New York, I'd been a fairly well-behaved, white, middle-class, suburban, Italian, Roman Catholic boy. I had supportive parents, a loving family, and by most measurements a young man's dream childhood, filled with pool parties, pizza binges, playground football, farting contests, spontaneous backyard campouts—and epic air-guitar battles. When I think about those days now, I recall laughing a lot, paying way too much attention to comic books, neighborhood girls, and rock stars, and generally feeling safe and secure in my cozy little half-frozen corner of the world.

Being both Italian *and* Catholic meant that I was raised on gluten and guilt. I had lots of pasta and lots of repentance (and decades later I still have a healthy appetite for both). As is true for so many of my tribe, our kitchen was a holy place, the continually simmering heart of our family. It was a place of sustenance and communion and belonging, thick with the sweet aroma of basil and frying meatballs and the sound of Frank Sinatra. From an early age, religion, rules, and rituals were the bedrock of our weekly family routine, woven into my daily studies and athletics and even my social life, by parents who valued the structure and moral values they hoped this would instill in me. As a result, faith formed the steady background noise of my daily life, with God always hovering overhead like the Spirit over the water at Creation—or maybe more like a stern, matronly grandmother making sure you washed properly. Either way, my hands stayed clean and I didn't cuss all that much.

For as long as I could remember, I had two really great stories planted within my heart, stories that not everyone has. The first was the story of a family that loved me. They spent time with me, told me that I mattered, that I was adored, that I could be anything I dreamed of being—and that they were *for* me. Home was a sanctuary. It was belonging. It was a soft place for my soul to find rest. Second, I had a story about God. In my God story, God was real, God was good, and I was fearfully and wonderfully made in the image of this very good God. (Admittedly this was a particularly tough sell during puberty and middle school breakups.) My faith story told me that God was massive and made everything, yet this same God knew me intimately and loved me completely. It was and is a beautiful and (I believe) true story, one that for most of my life has yielded the awareness that I was never alone and that God was always present. This realization has been at times comforting and at other times terrifying, depending on the day and my agenda.

Yet along with my stories about a big God who loved little me, and an affectionate family who was for me, I also inherited some *false* stories too, about people of color, about gay people, about poor people, about addicts, about born-again Christians, about atheists. In my handed-down narratives, these people were all to be avoided or feared, or at the very least approached with great skepticism, because something about the stories I'd learned told me that I was just a little bit more deserving of the love of this big God than they were. Some of these folks I looked at with pity and others with contempt, but I saw them *all* as surely undeserving of the close proximity to God that I as his favorite son had been blessed with. Most of us are raised in a similarly self-centered faith story, asking, "If God is for me, who can be against me?" and assuming that there is some competition with others that we are required to win in order to secure our acceptance. Such thinking forces us to quickly become experts at exclusion and at crafting a God who plays favorites. This is far easier when everything around you tells you that your skin color, gender, or orientation guarantee your place at the table.

My story told me that I was a beloved child and those whose lives were seemingly foreign to me were at best barely tolerated foster children who needed to do some work in order to earn a seat. I couldn't have described it that way then, but I remember how it felt to think about God and to count myself close and cared for, while believing so many others remained distant and disregarded. The truth I would later come to learn was that I was just another begging roadside leper who wrongly imagined himself a righteous Pharisee. False stories and small tables will do that every time. In fact, the source of the greatest dissonance in the modern Church is the belief that there are clearly defined insiders and outsiders; that God is somewhere *up there* keeping score like a cosmic Santa Claus, and we all need to figure out how to separate people into allies and adversaries, lest we align ourselves with the damned and not the saved, and guarantee our damnation.

These faulty biographies handed down to me weren't the result of targeted, sinister indoctrination by the adults around me or delivered through any specific verbal instruction. They were simply the predictable by-product of being around people who looked and talked and believed the way that they did. When this happens, your table is going to be small. That's what uniformity usually breeds: an inherited affinity for the familiar and a fear of what isn't. When the table you're used to sitting at is small, so too is your understanding of those seated elsewhere. Over time I'd quietly developed a subtly narcissistic religious worldview where God gradually became the *God of the Good People*, and conveniently the "good people" tended to always look and sound and believe an awful lot like I did. This was my spiritual incubator during the first eighteen years or so of my journey, and for most of that time it worked for me. Privilege usually works for those who have it, unless they are so roused that they are able to see with fresh eyes and notice their blind spots and the great advantage in their experience. Like a stain on the back of your shirt: you usually can't easily see your privilege and you need good, honest people around you to tell you—and then you need to listen.

Sometimes life tries to teach you and you have the good fortune to be paying attention. Age can illuminate things that used to be in shadow. The older you get, the more clearly you see that *all* of us are the products of our individual stories: the place we're born, the home of our youth, the experiences we have, the education we receive, and the people who frequently speak into our lives. Our specific, never-to-be-duplicated history shapes the way we see the world, the way we understand ourselves, the way we think about God. In both beautiful and disappointing ways, this had been my story. It came with blessings and liabilities that were mine alone. Although I had an image of a God who was towering and loving and present, I had a view of the world that was frighteningly narrow, where far too many people were disqualified from intimacy with that God. I wasn't a bad kid, I was just misinformed. Chances are, had I stayed where I was geographically, I would have continued to be loved and encouraged and cared for. I would have remained comfortably nestled in the narrative of my childhood and had that story reinforced by people who genuinely treasured me. I would have probably become a fairly decent, responsible adult with a tidy, albeit terribly selective narrative about the world—and my table would have stayed far too small for the God I claimed to believe in. Then God gave me Philadelphia. Hallelujah.

When you win a goldfish at the fair by tossing a ping-pong ball into his tiny bowl, you know you can't just dump the poor thing from his cozy little temporary Ziploc home and into a massive tank, because the system shock will likely kill him. Too much change too soon is a certain death sentence, and so you need to gradually ease the little guy into the bigger world, or that world will quickly overwhelm him and invariably leave him permanently swimming sideways—and you'll be flushing your newly earned trophy down the toilet. Thirty years ago I was a wide-eyed, suburban goldfish dropped from thirty thousand feet, straight into the churning heart of Philadelphia's murky Schuylkill River. Looking back, it's difficult to comprehend how my head didn't simply explode upon arrival at the corner of Broad and Pine, but I suppose this is what *grace* actually looks like, practically speaking. It allows you to find quite tolerable, even enjoyable, what might otherwise kick the living snot out of you. As my feet first hit the rugged, blistered pavement of the City of Brotherly Love, I stepped unexpectedly into a waiting Technicolor ambush of God-sized diversity, and though I couldn't know it then, my table was about to be expanded and my calling about to be born. Had I realized it all at the time, I would have removed my shoes, because these loud, weathered streets were indeed most holy ground. The ordinary always is.

I had no aspirations to be a pastor in these days, no inkling that ministry was even an option. In truth, I was at best a hopeful agnostic, barely having anything resembling a working faith except a few randomly strung-together remnants from my childhood Catholicism: stubborn, sacred holdouts loosely strewn through an ever-growing disbelief. On a scholarship to the University of the Arts as a graphic design major, I was suddenly surrounded by and living among artists, musicians, dancers, and actors, for most of whom theology was a late, lingering afterthought if it was a thought at all. This wasn't *church* as I recognized it, but it was a decidedly bohemian alternative congregation, where I regularly began working out my big-boy faith with fear, trembling—and lots of cheesesteaks. There were no Bible study groups or Sunday worship services or midweek prayer meetings, none of the familiar trappings of religion that I'd grown up with, but stuff was happening in me

just the same—deep, fundamental, soul-renovating stuff. Back
then, from the outside I would have probably been what modern traditional Christian culture identifies as *unchurched*: nonreligious, lost, and needing to be rescued. In the all-or-nothing
battle lines that the modern Church has carved out, my lack
of participation in a recognized local faith community would
have ensured this label. But labels rarely do justice to those on
whom we affix them.

In the eyes of the faithful, I was simply off God's grid. But
the deeper truth was not as easily distinguished. I couldn't even
see it myself at the time, but the place was absolutely teeming
with the things of God: the pungent bouquet of brightly col-
ored gobs of oil paint slathered across canvases, the rhythmic
stomps of synchronized dancers' feet hitting the hardwood stu-
dio floors, the meandering harmonies of impromptu choirs rising from the stairwells to mix with the street noise outside—a
jazz fusion of humanity that Miles Davis would've marveled at.
There was creativity and discovery and collaboration, and some
of the most authentic community I'd ever known or would
ever know. I realize now that this wasn't just an inner-city
art school; it was a covert cathedral wrapped in concrete and
fluorescent lights, a strikingly diverse masterpiece by Divinity's hand, even if I couldn't recognize it or name it at that
time. During those first weeks I spent glorious nights perched
on high-rise balconies with new friends talking about life and
love and the future. I began living alongside people whom my
story had previously kept at a safe distance. And with every
new relationship and every stereotype-busting exchange, I was
slowly being pulled from the tiny, climate-controlled Ziploc-
bag bubble of my childhood God story and into a wide expanse
that would make way for what was coming. My soul was being
tilled like rich, hard-packed soil in preparation for something
new and beautiful to grow, something far greater than what I
had understood religion to be and something far more suited
to the One who I had been taught spoke the very planet into
being and who gave consent for my very heart to begin beating. Philadelphia was giving me a crash course in the stunning

breadth and creativity of the maker of color, light, and sound. God was using a wonderfully odd collection of painters and piano players and comic book artists to rewrite my story. I was in the middle of a stunning plot twist—and was largely oblivious to it all. I just knew it was beautiful.

Turns out that this was Jesus' vision of the world too: life as cathedral. He moved through the streets and fields and homes of Palestine reminding people of the staggering glory that was beneath their feet and around their tables. He called people's attention to a "kingdom of heaven" that was in their midst if they could only become aware of it. It was a holistic understanding of divinity, where nothing was untouched by the hand of God; one where, as the apostle Paul would later describe, everyone was a living church, a breathing sanctuary (1 Cor. 3:16–17). Our modern understanding of spirituality is a far more binary endeavor, strictly dividing the world into the sacred and the secular, into religious life (which usually happens in a building for an hour on Sunday) and life outside religion (usually the other, more fun stuff). This makes building a bigger table a real challenge.

Things outside my college campus were no less revelatory, no less jarring, no less disorienting to my previously cloistered religious operating system. Philadelphia offered a free master class in beautiful, messy diversity. My first off-campus apartment was just off of Broad Street right in the loud, crackling heart of things, and my second-floor window overlooking Pine Street gave me the perfect perch to watch the daily ragamuffin parade. I had a front-row seat to life beyond the edges of the small table of my youth and childhood religion, as if I'd reached the edge of an old world and was blazing a trail to something previously untouched in my mind and heart. I may as well have been an alien because everything felt foreign to me, but in the best possible way. It's true that a change of environment gives you new eyes to view the world through, and I was seeing like never before. During my first year there I spent countless hours meandering through the city, over the weathered cobblestones from the first days of our nation as they intersected swaths of scalding, freshly paved asphalt. In the same block I'd pass pristine, hundred-year-old brownstones, nondescript Chinese restaurants, surprising preserved green spaces, and hand-painted murals on repurposed shuttered storefronts. *This* was the city I was falling in love with in its completeness: not a series of sharply delineated separate entities to be received on their own, but a stunning, continuous mosaic of disparate pieces that together made something new. Without *any* of those pieces it would cease to be the community that it was; its true identity was fashioned from that very specific diversity on display.

What I stepped into there each day was stark-naked *life*, stripped of the glossy veneer of my suburban past; jagged-edged, urine-soaked, graffiti-tagged, unsanitized reality I'd never experienced before. I found myself to be a new, tiny, irregular piece shoved awkwardly in a massive mosaic of need and affluence, of diverse dialects and unfamiliar spices, of street vendors and corner prostitutes, of young families and elderly beggars—and I found every second of it thrilling, if not regularly terrifying. I rubbed elbows with people I had no previous frame of reference for and began to wake up to the common ground in our shared humanity. I witnessed violence and poverty not as isolated news stories, but as the regular rhythm of the daily painful existence many people had to experience as their normal, one that I'd never imagined. It all began slowly softening my heart and breaking into new places in my brain, laying the foundation for the kind of pastor I would one day aspire to become—an *all-people* pastor.

I earned money my freshman year working at the university's café. For a lifelong foodie with a high metabolism and a low budget, this job was a perfect storm of pure goodness. I was able to help prepare amazing meals and to interact with students and faculty each afternoon working the front end. My dad's salesman genes were allowed to come to full fruition in me, and the counter provided a kind of stage where I could daily dispense one-liners, make people laugh, and in general offer the kind of gregarious hospitality that he had instilled in me, bolstered by a shared work ethic in which we both took tremendous pride. Every day I got the chance to literally welcome people to the table and to serve them well. It gave me great satisfaction to be a kind presence in their lives each day, and I loved being affectionately referred to as Café John around campus. In fact, I always felt a little like I was getting away with something by being paid for this gig—and regularly taking home chafing dishes filled with lasagna was a pretty nice bonus too.

Joe and Danny ran the café, which also catered the university's gallery receptions and fund-raising dinners. They'd hired both me and my freshman roommate Pete, and the two of them were excellent bosses to us, with that delicate balance of warmth and discipline that knows when to keep things loose and when to rein them in. We pumped a lot of food out of that tiny, stifling kitchen and we laughed hysterically in the process. There I learned the importance of creating a culture where people could do their best work, of hiring talented folks and releasing them to do what they were uniquely capable of doing. When someone really loves their work in any walk of life it shows, and both Joe and Danny seemed to revel in the work we all did together. Sure it was their livelihood, but it was a kind of ministry too, even if they didn't quite frame it that way. They were setting the table and feeding people. Their efforts were meeting people's physical needs along with attending to their spirits. I've always believed that anything done with care and joy can be an act of worship, and the kitchen for me has often been a form of church, even if the anointing oil in this case was olive.

A few weeks into my new job I remember thinking to myself, "Joe and Danny are *really* great friends. They run this business together, they hang out all the time, and I think they even bought a house together—what pals!" I did everything except channel one of my Italian aunts and hope out loud that they would both "find a nice girl one day." Clearly my cozy, suburban bubble upbringing was in full effect, as evidenced by my utter naiveté and relative oblivion in the moment. I don't remember exactly when Pete and I realized that not only were they a couple—but nearly the entire rest of the café staff was gay as well. We were straight and in the decided minority, but fortunately they were all much more gracious than straight folks tend to be with the roles reversed, and most certainly kinder than the Church. They treated us with the same respect and compassion and irreverent humor they greeted the rest of the staff with and made us feel as though we belonged. It's funny how little it takes to show people they matter and what a difference it makes in inviting them into meaningful community. Kindness, it turns out, is powerfully disarming.

I confess that had I known prior to being offered the job that I would be surrounded by gay men, there's a good chance I wouldn't have accepted it. I would have immediately transposed the poorly drawn, fear-fueled caricature of homosexuality that I grew up with onto them and rationalized my way out of the situation, satisfied that I had somehow made God happy. It was a spiritual truth for me back then that separation from "sinners" was a valid moral stance that proved *my* virtue and highlighted *others'* wrongdoing. Creating space between myself and other human beings was somehow a perfectly Christian response to difference, and if I'd had the opportunity up front, I'd have taken it. I would have squirmed through a brief awkward conversation, declined the job, and left feeling like I had dodged a bullet, when in reality I would have missed God giving me a chance to expand my table. I would have sidestepped blessings in the name of my religion.

But by the time I realized, a month into the job, that Joe and Danny shared monogrammed towels, we had already spent hours together, working, talking, fighting, laughing— and we had become family. I loved these guys. They were more than theoretical examples to be debated. They were not hot-button issues or some conveniently framed moral argument that I could make snap judgments about from a safe distance. Upon closer examination, Joe and Danny and the rest of the staff were simply *people*: people I was glad that I knew and who reflected God as clearly as anyone who passed in front of that counter each day—certainly as much as any I'd shared a church pew with back home. Their gender identity and sexual orientation made them no less image bearers of the Divine; their love was a reflection of the heart of God, not because of *who* they loved but because of *how* they loved—deeply, truthfully, and sacrificially.

The heart is a rather curious entity. Once its doors swing wide open, they can't easily be shut again. Meeting Joe and Danny had knocked the padlock off of a carefully guarded place in mine. They'd shown me that people we assume we don't have a great deal in common with are to be known and not feared. I'd reached a peaceful clearing in my previously fenced-in, heavily fortified worldview, a place I would return to again and again in my desire to be an *all-people* pastor, with varying degrees of success and failure.

Years later as a pastor, I would look and advocate for that same openness and variety in the Church and all too often find instead gentrified, sanitized, homogeneous faith communities that edited out those deemed too ragged, too left of center, or too difficult to deal with. It would be a carefully monitored and strictly policed diversity that professed to reflect heaven but more often simply reflected suburbia, with all the rough-edged people sandblasted smooth by doctrine and dogma until they were palatable enough to keep around or hid their junk or disappeared altogether. I would come to find that the openness during these days in Philadelphia that served me so well would eventually become a liability as I stepped deeper into ministry. It would be seen as a deficiency in the eyes of superiors and peers who wanted a palatable version of diversity, one that they could control, one that fit comfortably and behaved well in a one-hour worship service. The expansive table of hospitality growing in me here would eventually have to be sawed down substantially if I wanted it to fit through the church doors, because despite all our talk about seeking *all people*, the truth is we religious folk usually favor a far more selective sampling.

If I'd been at all familiar with the life and ministry of Jesus then I'd have been better prepared for this, as the fight to widen the parameters of those invited into redemptive community was his daily work. The Pharisees, the religious leaders of Jesus' Jewish tradition, always saw the table as growing too big, because their sole deservedness had been sewn into them from birth by their faith story, not unlike the narrative of white evangelicals in America exploited in our recent presidential campaign, where the fear of the other was leveraged to keep the table not only small, but also well-guarded. Jesus warns his disciples not to allow this self-centered, fear-saturated teaching of the religious elite to contaminate our understanding of the diversity around us or to create in us contempt for those who seem to stand opposite us politically, theologically, or socially (Matt. 16:5–12; 23:13).

I'd soon figure out the nuanced politics of pastoring and learn how to broker a tenuous, fragile truce between the minister I *wanted* to be and the one I was *expected* to be. I'd learn how to navigate the pew-sitting "shareholders" on whose approval my job security and financial stability both rested. As I would build up an equity of trust in the community, I would learn what I could and couldn't say and how far I could stretch people theologically before they snapped—or snapped back. And eventually I would find myself beyond that point to gloriously disastrous effect on my career, but for now as a young, hopeful agnostic artist roaming the City of Brotherly Love with no religious aspirations to speak of. I was seeing just how big the table could and should be—the one I'd later give everything to build as a pastor. It was the gathering place where strippers and gay caterers and atheists all had a standing invitation, not to receive charity from someone morally superior and not to serve as religious projects to be converted and fixed—but as welcome dinner guests of a hospitable Jesus who modeled what happens when we break bread with the broken: we find ourselves there too.

2

When in Rome

Worlds are made in six days, so imagine what can happen in four months.

That's how long I'd been in Rome for a semester of art school, studying and living in the shadow of the Vatican. For a budding artist and foodie, Italy is about as close as one can get to heaven while still staying connected to one's body. I'd spent my days that summer meandering down stone-covered roads, stumbling into unassuming churches filled with stunning masterpieces I'd known my whole life only from textbooks. I remember seeing everything with constant wonder and being daily overwhelmed with how much beauty could be packed into the small space of these tiny, ancient streets. As usually happens when you leave home, I was absorbed in my surroundings and didn't consider that eventful stuff could possibly be going on back there to rival my experiences. Little did I know that my brother had dropped a bombshell so big that I should have felt the tremors all the way at the Vatican.

Not much appeared to have changed when I arrived back at my childhood home in Central New York, other than the September foliage now brilliantly afire and visible outside every window. I'd only been home for an hour or so when my mother called upstairs from the kitchen.

"John, . . . come down here."

I recognized something different in her voice. Live with people long enough, and in only a word you can tell when something's up—and something absolutely was. As I bolted down the stairs I quickly did a mental inventory of elderly relatives, certain I was about to be alerted of the demise of one of them. I braced myself for her news. When I reached the kitchen, my mother was standing at the sink, looking out the window. "What's going on?" I asked buoyantly, but not at all sure I wanted to know. She turned and paused for what seemed like minutes and finally said it flatly, without buffer or fanfare: "Your brother is gay."

It's amazing how many things can flood in and out of your mind in a matter of a few seconds, how all the questions, thoughts, memories, and contingencies can create a funnel-cloud swirl inside your head in the span of a breath. So many emotions crammed themselves into that second, but the one that crowded out the rest was relief. My face might have shown surprise, but within an instant, so much about those four words just made sense. My brother had struggled with depression and with episodes of behavior that seemed out of place with the effervescent, silly boy we'd always known him to be. My brother had always been one of the funniest people on the planet for my money, but for a long time he'd seemed to have lost some of his joy. (As it turns out, not being able to be the most authentic version of yourself can wreak havoc with your insides and leave you not feeling much like laughing.) Struggling as we had been to make sense of my brother's recent sadness, his revelation now wasn't as much the unexpected explosion that it might be for many families; it was more like the discovery of a long-missing puzzle piece. This was in fact what it was: the return of the wholeness that comes with being able to be the truest *you* there is.

Though I'd missed the dramatic moment in that same kitchen just a month earlier when my brother first shared the news with everyone, it gave me great joy to later hear that it perfectly reflected the warmth and humor that has always characterized my family. After a fair bit of tears and volume (things that were not uncommon in our kitchen on most ordinary days), and blessedly a unanimous expression of unwavering love, my mother leaned against the kitchen counter and began to cry. My father looked up at her and said, "What the hell are you crying about?" She replied through sobs, "I just want him to be happy!" My father then turned to my brother and said with a wry smile, "Don't be happy, son—be gay!" As was so often his way, my father used humor to say something he could say no other way, and what he was saying to my brother and to all of us was that we were still the same family. For as much as the news might have altered some things, nothing was going to alter this. This conversation shaped the path forward for my brother and for our entire family. It set the tone for who we would be and what we would tolerate from others. We had a bigger table there in that kitchen than we'd ever had before. I was never more proud of my family.

Many people think that having someone close to you come out clouds your vision, but in reality it clarifies it. It redefines words for you. It rewrites false stories. It renovates your religion. It forces you to understand sexuality not as some detached issue but as what it is—human beings; in this case, those you know and love dearly. This is the gift relationship gives you. That proximity we get to people will always show us what we couldn't see any other way. When you are faced with the reality of having an LGBTQ family member or close friend, it forces you to hold up your theology to see what it's really made of. And when this happens, some of it gets confirmed, some of it gets shifted, and some of it gets blown up. I'd already done my homework. I'd studied. I'd prayed through it. I'd already reconciled so many of my feelings on gender identity and sexual orientation before this moment, so I knew without blinking that I didn't have to choose between loving God and loving my brother—and he didn't have to choose between being gay and being adored by God.

One of the things you learn when you walk down the path of being an ally is that people aren't LGBTQ based on the consent you give or don't give to them, the approval you provide or withhold. That's not how gender identity and sexual orientation work. Your acceptance doesn't give people permission to be anything. It simply allows them to be fully authentic in your presence and to feel loved as they are. It secures people in those places where they should feel fully secured: in their families and friendships and workplaces and churches. If you don't think you have LGBTQ family members, coworkers, classmates, and friends right now, you may want to ask yourself if that's because you've created an environment in which they would be afraid to share it even if they were. It might be that your words and manner have already told people that they're not safe to be honest with you. As our society thankfully becomes less and less hostile to the LGBTQ community and as people begin to gradually feel safer in authenticity, more children will come out and more families will have a new reality to reckon with. Those families will continue to seek spiritually and they will continue to need and deserve to be in faith communities where they are fully welcomed. It is one of the reasons the table needs to be made bigger.

I know that for many people of faith, maybe even for you, LGBTQ acceptance is still, in a very real way, a spiritual world rocker. I pray that if you are unsure how to respond to someone who comes out to you, you'll take a cue from my father, who—despite all he didn't know or understand in the moment—didn't feel a pressing need to lecture, preach, or answer every question. He simply made sure that his love was the loudest thing he spoke. He didn't realize it then, but he was showing me Jesus in a way that surprised and inspired and transformed me.

Friend, the heart of the bigger table is the realization that we don't have to share someone's experience to respect their road. As we move beyond the lazy theology and easy caricatures that seek to remove any *gray* from people's lives, we can meet them in that grayness, right where they are, without demanding that they become something else in order to earn proximity to us or to a God who loves them dearly. Just as was true in the life and ministry of Jesus, real love is not contingent upon alteration; it simply is. There is no earning of fellowship or deserving of closeness; there is only the invitation itself and the joy that comes when you are fully seen and fully heard. When in Rome, you shouldn't need to do as the Romans do in order to be welcomed. You are already welcomed.

Examples abound of churches and pastors limiting their welcome and being stingy with their invitations to the table, but thankfully we know many other Christians who are always ready to set a new place or two. It was one such pastor and congregation that brought me back to the church and ultimately changed my life.

After meeting in college, my wife-to-be and I had found our way to a little country Methodist church in the suburbs just west of Philadelphia, where we had been living. As far away as the two of us were at the time from organized (or even slightly disorganized) religion, planning our wedding ceremony had triggered the muscle memory of our childhood faith, stirring up within both of us the idea of church again, of inviting God into the occasion and into our marriage in some "official" way. We were both feeling drawn back to faith, yet each of us was apprehensive about sharing it with the other for fear of making waves and messing up a good thing this late in the game. One afternoon, I finally floated out a fragile trial balloon. "Maybe we should just have a church wedding!" I said almost sarcastically as a preemptive defense strategy, should things go badly.

"I think we should," my fiancée said.

And just like that, we started the road back.

It had been years since either of us had been part of a local faith community, so we began our path-altering journey the way one did pre-Internet—we opened up the phone book. I remember meandering through the Yellow Pages with no real discernment process other than determining reasonable distance from our home and calling churches to see who would be willing to marry two backsliding believers currently living in sin. The response was less than enthusiastic. Few churches called us back, and those that did had a laundry list of requirements and bureaucratic hoops to jump through before we could begin the conversation, most of which felt more than a little intimidating from the outside. One phone call was different, though. This church's pastor personally called me back. Her name was Susan May. I remember being shocked to be speaking directly with a pastor, let alone a female one. My younger Catholic schoolboy self could never have conceived of such a thing. She was soft-spoken and kind, and after listening to our story for a few minutes she said, "Why don't you come visit us this Sunday, and if you have a good experience we can talk more?" I wrote down her name and the service times on a yellow sticky note. I still have it. It's a kind of sacred relic to me now of my journey toward the bigger table.

It had been a long time since we had stepped into a house of worship, and never into one that wasn't Catholic, save for a wedding or funeral here or there. Our first Sunday at the Methodist church felt a little like I was cheating on the faith of my youth. I imagined alarms going off at my family priest's home that morning in Central New York and an unmarked car being dispatched to retrieve me. (Guilt is a heck of a drug.) It was one of those ubiquitous white chapels seating no more than one hundred or so, adorned only by red shutters and a simple cross. Inside, plain wrought-iron light fixtures and rows of smooth, weathered pews lined the space. It was completely unassuming, but I was nervous nonetheless. When inside you feel like an outsider, that happens. I've never forgotten how disorienting it was to be new in church, and just how difficult it can be walking through those doors when your confidence or faith is shaken. I soon realized I didn't need to be worried. Within seconds the butterflies departed from our bellies, the fears subsided, and we felt as though we'd come home. The feeling of close community, which had evaded me in my previous church experience, was so very apparent there, almost instantly. There was something about that place and those people that over those first few weeks began to fill in the holes we'd had about the Church, giving us something tangible to hold onto and helping us to believe for the first time in a long time that we might not be finished with this religion thing just yet. We felt seen and known and loved without needing to prove ourselves worthy. There's nothing like that feeling.

I've never forgotten the impact of that first phone conversation with Pastor May. If she'd had the same rigid understanding of religion so many others had, she might have been less hospitable or less sensitive to the voice on the other end of the line—and our road would have been completely different. I would have never felt at ease enough to enter that church (let alone volunteer with teenagers) and certainly never been compelled to leave my life's work a year or so later to become a full-time pastor. Thankfully Pastor May had a heart prepared to receive me that day. This is how simple and yet profoundly powerful the act of expanding the table can be. One phone call. One word of kindness. One small, open door. It can even be destination changing.

People often like to talk about entering ministry as a getting a "tap on the shoulder." I always figured they were talking metaphorically. During our first months in that tiny church I experienced a renaissance in my spirit, a new momentum altering my path in small but decided steps. I began to feel lighter and more hopeful. Things were changing, but I never anticipated what would happen one November Sunday. The service came to a close, and as we spoke the final Amen, I was already processing where we'd be having lunch and considering whether or not the Eagles' outside pressure could get to the Giants' quarterback. Before I could pull myself out of the pew, I felt a hand upon my shoulder. (Not the figurative hand of God, but an actual human hand.) I turned and my eyes met the warm smile of a woman I'd come to know as an enthusiastic regular there named Karen. After we exchanged greetings and made some benign small talk, she pulled a little closer, looked me directly in the eyes, and said, "John, I've been thinking about you and praying about you, and I think you'd make an amazing youth leader."

I immediately thought to myself, "I know you. You're the current youth leader!"

Karen had already done her time, paid her debt to society, and was looking to get out and start her new life. (Ministry, I'd eventually learn, can do that to you.) My wife and I fit all the criteria to lead the youth group of a small church: we were young, married, and we had no criminal record (at least no felonies that they were aware of). At that time my faith was the very smallest of fragile embers. I really hadn't owned my evolving spirituality yet. I certainly had little desire to minister and even fewer qualifications to do so, but the church wasn't asking for any. My yes was enough for them. Turns out I would find God to work the very same way: our ability isn't as important as our availability. You start with an uninformed, enthusiastic yes, and you begin walking. God requires that and little more.

I thought about Karen's invitation for a few seconds, quickly scanned my wife's face for signs of panic, and finding none there, in that creaky country church pew, in a perfect example of missing the incredible power often present in a seemingly ordinary moment, I said, "Sure!" Not six hours later we found ourselves hanging out with a handful of middle and high school students in a space much like the youth-group rooms in most old, small churches in America: a moldy, Cold War–era basement littered with discarded couches of questionable patterning, some water-damaged posters with Scripture verses, a half-dozen largely beanless beanbags, and the requisite partially working foosball table. The place was continually flooded, regularly invaded by rodents, and probably not legally fit for actual human occupation, but it was the holiest of grounds, the sacred spot where God beautifully renovated us on a regular basis. There was no show, no event, no sexy lure, just the handful of us and the God of the big table. It's something I would strive to hold onto as the buildings would become larger, the budgets exponentially greater, the productions more professional, and as I felt more prepared and competent: Ministry isn't about conjuring up the presence of God; it's about removing the distractions to realizing that presence has been there all the time. In noisy, overfilled days, the best ministry is always going to be subtraction.

It's hard to quantify my experience in that mildewed bunker with those students, but when you're in the sweet spot of your calling, you just know it. I felt more like myself than I'd felt in a long time. On that night and those that followed, something was released within me; a long-closed-off room had been suddenly unlocked, allowing me to access a gift and calling I hadn't realized was there: a heart for helping people, specifically teenagers. In conversations mixed with laughter and awkward silence, we were knit together. In messy games and over bad pizza and through thousands of rather uneventful moments, we became family. Even though I'd never led a class, Bible study, or youth meeting, I remembered enough from my own adolescence to know that teenagers smell manure a mile away. Their BS detectors are finely tuned, and they know when someone is being real and when they're peddling fecal matter. Teenagers have less experience pretending and have a far lower tolerance for it. They're not yet fully conditioned to censor themselves for the sake of acceptance, and they aren't looking for adults to either. They just want you to be yourself. The same, I would find, is not always true of the church at large.

3

Going against the Family

Organized religion and organized crime can be frighteningly similar at times. Both tend to rely on unwavering loyalty and on participants passionately defending their own. In ministry and in the Mafia, when things are going right you're well fed and fiercely loved, but make one bad move, cross one wrong person—and it's horse heads in the bed and concrete sneakers. In either house there's often a startlingly narrow line between a holy kiss and the kiss of death, and learning how to stay on the boss's good side becomes a matter of survival.

The Church can be a beautiful or horrifying place, depending on where you're standing. (As they say in real estate, location truly *is* everything.) We Christians know how to do love really well when we believe someone is on the inside, when they're one of us, part of our tribe—when they're *in the family*. There's a tangible sense of shared purpose and mutual affection that comes with being part of a local faith community, a feeling of belonging that really does transcend almost anything one can experience. Less than a year from that seemingly ordinary Sunday night when I led youth group for the first time, I found myself jumping from the job I'd spent my whole life preparing to get, because this new thing had seized my heart. When the Church is being its best, Christ-reflecting, barrier-destroying, table-expanding self, it's pretty difficult to beat for sheer fraternal belonging-ness and for making you feel like you're part of something greater than just you. In the local church I've been held in times of intense grieving, supported financially in difficult seasons, and had my family cared for in ways too great to measure. I've received forgiveness and encouragement and lavish love. There I've found my purpose, learned how to navigate adversity, and been given a front-row seat from which to view the work of God. The local church has been home for me. I believe in what the Church can and should be, and it's the reason I've shown up every week for the past twenty years: to try and provide this kind of hope-giving, life-sustaining community for people so starved for it.

The problem is that the deep familial bond that religion nurtures can so easily become toxic, so quickly be turned inside out when someone is perceived as somehow deviating too greatly in either behavior or belief: what a mob boss would call *going against the family*. The infractions precipitating such a schism are many: an expression of doubt, a changing theological conclusion, a momentary error in judgment. In the wake of such things, people can instantly find themselves pushed to the periphery of the community or separated altogether, with very little warning or due process—and the long road back can be brutal. Millions of people who once participated in organized Christianity and who no longer do can testify to this. Ask people about their exodus from the Church and many will tell you stories of their forced estrangement, of becoming reluctant prodigals wanting desperately to return home and no longer welcomed back. They will talk about being shunned, disconnected, silenced—made persona non grata in the place where they were once told they were welcomed as they were, and had felt as much. They'll share how quickly they were made to feel dead to a group of people who had given them so much life, and the way their faith had nearly been killed along with it.

It is into this uniquely treacherous space of both great danger and possibility that the pastor steps. Had I known this earlier, I probably would have sprinted in the opposite direction, but perhaps God gave me the gift of temporary ignorance, just long enough to say yes. After a year of volunteer ministry at a suburban Philadelphia church, I began attending a local seminary and soon found myself on the church's staff, now paid to be a pastor. Living and working in the center of this tension in an official capacity was an occupational hazard I was unprepared for. The unfolding weeks became a crash course in learning how to navigate the intricate web of relationships among lots of people who were, ironically, finally finding belonging, yet still themselves wired for exclusion. I was stewarding saved sinners rejoicing in an unmerited grace that they themselves were so prone to be stingy with. Religion tends to leverage fear in the name of community, to magnify the barrier between it and the world around it, and as a result the local church has a propensity to become more parochial, more defensive, and more insular if not continually pushed outward. The gravitational pull toward self-preservation and self-absorption is incredibly strong, especially on pastors and church staff when they come to understand that the people in their care are also their shareholders, those who pay their salaries and control their job security, and in this way can yield great power over their personal convictions.

When I was still a "civilian" in the Church, it never occurred to me just how much those in ministry can allow their prophetic voices to be gradually buried beneath the expectations of the congregation, and just how political a process ministering in such a public way can become. Despite their claims of gracious hospitality, churches are often far more aggressive than they'd like to admit. Regardless of our language about being part of the greater body of Christ, the truth is that most local faith communities feel that they are doing religion better, smarter, more biblically, more faithfully than everyone else—most especially the other churches in the neighborhood. In this way, the table is almost always going to default to self-preservation, to competition rather than collaboration. Most pastors know the kind of attendance the churches around them are getting, the work they're doing in the community, the media coverage they're getting—and it matters to them. Churches talk about inviting all people, but more often than not they're just cannibalizing other local congregations while competing for the same target audience. They aren't extending to reach those who aren't already engaged in spiritual community as much as fine-tuning their methods to steal from their neighbors by offering better amenities. And instead of speaking or leading from a place of authenticity, instead of living from the quiet places of personal revelation outward, many pastors end up charged with simply building and maintaining a local brand, of keeping the peace and getting fannies in the seats—of growing and protecting the family. Such an environment is ripe for leadership duplicity.

There are many reasons the local church is so vulnerable to such all-or-nothing extremism; not least among them is the way so much of our Christianity has been immersed in relentless us-vs.-them culture-war rhetoric. Scaring people into the kingdom by enlisting them for combat has been the evangelical church in America's bread and butter for the past fifty years, and it's worked out pretty well. It's been a reliable way to generate urgency among the faithful and to get people worked up, but ultimately it's also been costly. Frame the spiritual journey as a stark good-vs.-evil battle of warring sides long enough and you'll eventually see the Church and those around you in the same way too. You'll begin to filter the world through the lens of conflict. Everything becomes a threat to the family; everyone becomes a potential enemy. Fear becomes the engine that drives the whole thing. When this happens, your default response to people who are different or who challenge you can turn from compassion to contempt. You become less like God and more like the Godfather. In those times, instead of being a tool to fit your heart for invitation, faith can become a weapon to defend yourself against the encroaching sinners threatening God's people—whom we conveniently always consider ourselves among. Religion becomes a cold, cruel distance maker, pushing from the table people who aren't part of the brotherhood and don't march in lockstep with the others.

After a few years in Philadelphia, we began what would be a long season of ministry in the southeastern Bible Belt, which would provide another system shock to my Yankee religious sensibilities. I can remember the first time I felt like I hadn't just taken a new job but unknowingly joined the Mafia. I'd been on staff in a large megachurch for only a few months. We were in a lay leadership meeting when one of my coworkers matter-of-factly blurted out, "Everyone knows no self-respecting Christian can actually be a Democrat!" There seemed to be complete and quite passionate agreement around the circle, with several choice editorial comments offered. (Apparently I hadn't gotten the memo in seminary.) Further commentary on the "gay agenda" followed, and I could feel my face getting hotter. I wanted to respond, but I was just self-aware enough and just green enough to keep my mouth shut while boiling over internally. Rather than offering a rebuttal, I acquiesced. Instead of speaking a dissenting voice into the discussion, I yielded to the room and to the status quo. It was my first taste of the way the deep connection in the Church can encourage its resisting the bigger table and of how easy it is to be complicit in it. I began to realize how much our desire for community can hinder our willingness to be authentic, especially when the consensus seems not in our favor.

We religious folk seem to need our deal breakers, our litmus-test issues and categories and stances that help us identify our common enemy and separate ourselves from them. These imagined adversaries help rally people together and help forge the very fierce familial bond we experience in the Church that can feel so life-giving when we're there. And this only works as long as the world is sharply delineated in stark black and white, with the good and bad guys clearly defined. It's why so often in the Church today, our points of differences, political affiliations, theological positions, and social stances, which *could* expand the table of our understanding, all become so divisive and so polarizing—because we need them to be to keep the battle lines visibly drawn. The narrative of our rare goodness and the evil horde threatening it requires this war rhetoric and this fear posture to stay alive. To endure any differences in such a desperate spiritual warfare environment feels like a defeat. Compromise becomes a mortal sin, and so we wear our intolerance for the manufactured *other* like a moral badge of honor. We double down on exclusion, certain that this is defending the faith.

The lack of theological diversity within local church communities and online communities is prohibiting the bigger table we *could* be creating there. Instead of learning to endure and bear with one another, we simply remove or further marginalize those with a minority view, requiring them to be silent or to move elsewhere and find another table. This is understandable if everything is done in allegiance to and fear of the Godfather (or rather, God the Father), only in religion, the threat isn't just getting knocked off—it's eternal damnation.

We're all looking for a way to judge our own moral worth, to quantify our goodness in our heads, to prove ourselves righteous to others, and so we survey the landscape and scan others' lives for those beliefs and behaviors by which we can declare them inferior from a distance. We live fully aware of our fatal flaws, but we can overlook those things when we need to. We can ignore our hypocrisy if it helps us tell a better story about us. We want the black and white and so we willingly ignore the fact that life is gray, that faith is gray, that we are gray. And the truth is, we all desperately want loving community, and we will be willing to do an awful lot to try and earn a place there.

There's a famous scene in *The Godfather Part II* where family boss Michael Corleone has discovered that his unscrupulous brother Fredo has turned traitor. In Michael's world, where loyalty is sacred, you simply don't go against the family and you don't get to fail more than once. Fredo pleads for mercy from his brother, but we know he isn't going to get it, and we're largely OK with this. Our family loyalty, our aversion to betrayal, is that strong. We want him to get what's coming to him, which is an easy position to take—as long as we don't see ourselves as Fredo. In that case, our knees hit the floor and we make the impassioned case for an exception. In this same way, most of us are fine worshiping two different Gods simultaneously. One we want to be endlessly patient with our vacillation, to forgive our broken promises and perpetual failures, to tolerate our defiance and doubts, to be always ready with another chance. In the face of our weaknesses and flaws we want for *ourselves* what Fredo wants from his brother Michael: compassion, forgiveness, and restoration. We want grace. We feel we deserve such things without caveat, and in those moments *this* is the God we choose to believe in. But when it comes to the sins of *other* people, we're far more willing to believe in a Maker who sends traitors to sleep with the fishes, who puts them on ice and makes them disappear without warning or reprieve. We seek for ourselves the kind of mercy that we are so very hesitant to give to those who cross us. We get our grace and they get damnation. We receive restoration and they get bumped off. This inconsistency is an ever-present danger for people of faith living in community with others.

One of the biggest, most damaging mistakes too many Christians so willingly make is assuming that God is as much of a judgmental jerk as we are. But what if we could make room for difference and space for disagreement in our spiritual communities? What if we could give permission for moral failure and freedom to not be certain, and the chance to gloriously fail without needing those things to become black marks against people or death-penalty offenses? What if we made space for people who are as screwed up as we are?

Growing up as a good Catholic boy, one of the things I dreaded more than dental work and Brussels sprouts was making the sacrament of confession. This is where you were supposed to regularly bare your sickly soul to the parish priest, sharing your darkest, most vile thoughts and deeds so that you could receive a fitting prayer penance and be forgiven. And it didn't always happen under the safe cover of a dark, heavily partitioned phone booth in the sanctuary (which was difficult enough), but often face-to-face, under the raking fluorescent light of a Sunday school classroom. There, we were expected to tell the guy who ran the church and represented God (and who knew our parents) about masturbation and porn and stealing and all the other stuff we wouldn't dare tell anyone else. Fortunately, I quickly learned as a ten-year-old how to handle such a heavy, existentially loaded proposition: I lied. Well, not exactly, but I did what most Christians end up doing in the church as adults. I learned how to manipulate the truth to save my behind. I'd crafted a handy, go-to list of "acceptable sins," benign stuff I could toss out to the priest without meriting an exorcism or a phone call to my parents. I'd cop to yelling at my brothers, being disrespectful to my parents—harmless things like that. It gave me the illusion of honesty without having to disclose the full breadth and depth of my adolescent depravity and the accompanying judgment and guilt it would certainly merit. I learned how to work the system by managing perception. I did what good brothers in the Mafia do: I kept my mouth shut.

This is what happens in far too many faith communities. There's a conspiracy of silence that Christians regularly take part in, a carefully controlled authenticity where we are *selectively* vulnerable, with just enough truth telling to ingratiate ourselves in the community but not so much that we unearth the really nasty stuff and end up on emergency prayer lists and in hastily assembled pastor meetings. Our churches often cultivate a heavily edited, carefully guarded openness and encourage others to do the same. We don't have truth, we have *church-sanctioned* truth, partial authenticity that will keep us on the inside and minimize the chances of our ostracism. Divorces, addiction struggles, moral lapses, depression, faith crises, and church conflicts all get crammed back down into the dark places, never brought fully into the light of community for fear of the consequences. The very areas of our deepest need and greatest struggle are often the most neglected. Our desire to stay in the family is so strong that we will gladly choose to conceal parts of our true selves over the full revelation that will get us expelled. It is on this fearful illusion of family that the Church so often gets built, and when the stinking reality of who we are finally *does* surface, it makes a huge mess because it seems so foreign, so exceptional—instead of feeling as commonplace as it actually is. Churches get leveled and relationships are severed, all because we didn't want to do the messy, costly work up front of sharing everything and admitting that maybe we're all family precisely because of our junk, that we're all in equal need of mercy, and that God is more benevolent and patient than we ever are with one another.

It didn't take long before I became more and more comfortable with the personal compromises I began to make as a pastor and family member, of hiding both my flaws and my fears. The sacrifice felt worth it, because this highly edited version of myself was cared for and affirmed and loved in our community. That's what the church of the small table looks like in the flesh: a group of well-meaning but carefully managed impostors, all sharing only those things they believe will secure their spot and sustain their inclusion—no one ever able to be fully real. That's what the family can do if we're not careful. You want so much to be a part of it that you'll stay silent when you feel compelled to speak, and you'll turn your head if what you see will be too painful or costly to confront. For a while I was OK with this. For a while I was a good soldier. For a while I was safe on the inside.

4

Earthquakes and Aftershocks

They say that earthquakes are one of the most frightening experiences a human being can endure. When the very ground beneath your feet becomes unstable, nothing feels safe anymore. There's nowhere to run away from the fear, no escape from the shaking. Similarly, when the bedrock of your religion starts to shift, it brings panic that is equally terrifying, equally disorienting. These seismic spiritual tremors can sometimes come as a singular event, some experience of profound pain or loss or injury that causes us to question the entire system in one catastrophic instant. We can see or pass through such trauma that the bottom of our belief seems to drop out without warning; the death of a loved one, a national tragedy, another's suffering can be precise moments when we lose our religion—though it is rarely that clear and identifiable. It's usually a matter of degrees. More often, the journey into an earth-rattling crisis of faith begins so quietly, unfolds so subtly and gradually, that we don't even realize it. We can't see the drifting until one day we turn around and see with great heartbreak how far we are from where we started, how distant God feels, and how little solid holy ground there seems beneath us. That place of uncertainty, especially if you're not used to standing on it, can be a nightmare. Deconstruction is hell.

Most of us like to think of our faith as a relatively solid thing; one singular, monolithic structure within which all our various spiritual pursuits are contained. We usually believe we have a compartmentalized religion, where we stuff things in and take things out as we need to, and the integrity of the bigger thing stays largely unaffected. But in reality belief is more like a Jenga tower, a series of interconnected pieces that moves and shifts, with each one supporting and depending upon all the other pieces to stand. It is the ever-moving sum total of our upbringing, study, prayer, experience, and every spoken or silent thought we've ever had about life and death and God. What that means is that nothing happens in our souls or in our belief systems independently of anything else despite what we think at any given moment. There are no isolated spiritual experiences. There is no issue that exists separated from everything else. No matter what we're dealing with in front of us, life is never about just *what it's about* on the surface and in the moment; there is always more happening, always a backstory that preceded the present crisis. Everything we believe, feel, and experience either sturdies us up or shakes us up in ways we can't prevent, even when we'd like to.

When we are in a period of growth or stability or joy, this interconnectedness is helpful because everything benefits. For example, as we experience a new understanding of God in our moments of quiet reflection, it might give us a greater hunger to engage the Scriptures. Or, if we experience transformation in meaningful community, we may feel compelled to be more open speaking about our personal faith with others. The work of the soul is a wonderful multiplier in this way. There is a *holy momentum* that we find ourselves in the grip of when we are living in a season of confidence, where our entire spirituality is strengthened. Faith begets faith. But when we sense something is faulty or cracks appear somewhere, the integrity of the whole thing is threatened, and collapse looms. Doubt, it turns out, begets doubt, too, which can be transformative or debilitating.

Our working theology is formed over and over again in the middle of this constant movement. For example, how we think about the Bible isn't just one of those interlocking pieces of our belief systems but it encompasses millions of them, and yet there is always one initial place, a seemingly inconsequential moment where we first create a disturbance.

For many people of faith, there are gateway issues: specific theological conflicts or moral dilemmas that cause us to reexamine what had always been givens in our religion. It may be the doctrine of hell or the nature of salvation or the institution of the Church or the inerrancy of Scripture or the mechanism of prayer. These seemingly isolated things can start us down the road of much larger scrutiny of our childhood faith. We begin to ask difficult questions of the assumptions we've always been expected to simply sign off on as part of membership in our particular spiritual club.

For me, the deconstruction began when I started to find that the traditional Christian theology regarding gender identity and sexual orientation no longer rang true. I knew what I knew about the LGBTQ community from my time in Philadelphia and the people I'd been led to there. I had the reality of my own family. I now had names and faces as clear, living rebuttals to the religion of my youth. I'd heard more accurate stories about gay people, had the table of my hospitality expanded—and it had altered me. The scales had been lifted from my eyes. Sometimes reality begins to argue with your theology. Your experience no longer matches your belief system and you stand in the precarious spot where those two things rub up against one another to tumultuous effect. I could no longer ignore the lazy, oversimplified interpretation of Scripture the Church often used to try and succinctly explain away what I knew to be the nuanced complexity of gender identity and sexual orientation. I started to dig deeper into the handful of Scripture passages, those "clobber verses"* I'd always been

*Gen. 19:1–11; Lev. 18:22; 20:13; Rom. 1:26–28; 1 Cor. 6:9–10; 1 Tim. 1:9–10 are known as the "clobber verses" of Scripture, used by nonaffirming Christians to justify prohibitions against the LGBTQ community.

told were so very clear on sexuality—and learned they were not. I could see how irresponsibly the Church has used these isolated texts to justify a sustained contempt for the LGBTQ community, how they've fueled the politicized religion we've adopted as gospel and perpetuated the horrible witness we're making in the culture on behalf of Jesus. I looked at organized Christianity's historic characterization and treatment of LGBTQ men and women, and I found no Jesus in it. None of it rang true anymore. None of it gave me any peace—not in my study, not in the pulpit, not in my solitary moments of prayer, and not living life alongside openly LGBTQ people for whom the word *abomination* could not be more ill fitting and demeaning.

As I began to do the work of examining a few Scriptures myself, I thought that was all I was doing. I naively figured that I could come to some tidy little conclusion about those disconnected verses and move forward with the rest of my theological structure largely unscathed. Digging deeper into that handful of passages about "the gay issue" seemed like a fairly benign and self-contained endeavor at the time, yet the more I studied and the further I moved into those verses of the text, the more unrest I felt. I could sense that I was doing more than just trying to better understand what the Bible said about the LGBTQ community. I was actually disrupting the entire tower.

This is how deconstruction begins: with one nagging question, with one uneasy feeling, with a single verse, with a solitary fear. And once it begins in earnest, it's terrifying, which is why so many Christians are content never looking at the Bible too closely or challenging a theological precept too forcefully—not because we don't feel such things are needed, but because we're afraid of the path they might lead us down. It's just easier and less taxing to take a pastor's word for it and act as though we're fine with that, operating on a sort of existential autopilot that stays safely in the superficial. We attempt to operate blissfully unaware of all that is not quite right and hoping that this will eventually right us. Following those deeper promptings, even though they might lead us to a truer truth, becomes something we resist with everything we have because we realize just how much work we might have to do, how much dead weight we might have to discard, and what a bomb it might set off in the bedrock of our faith. Most of us default to this position if we're not careful, enjoying the spiritual journey of least resistance.

Earlier, when I still believed the false stories I'd inherited, this theology was easy enough to tolerate and defend, because it reinforced the narrative I already believed about gay people and about what the Bible said about them and their "homosexual lifestyle." It didn't require me to push back or to do any work or examine the depth of my religious convictions, and this was attractive. I could fit comfortably into orthodoxy because it made my life easier. Now I had to deal with the internal shifting or ignore it altogether. I had to decide whether or not I could embrace the questions and live with the personal, existential, and career fallout. I had to decide whether I was going to listen to Jesus or to the Christianity I'd inherited, to yield to the Spirit within me or to the system around me. The path is often far less clear when you're standing in the middle of it. One of the most difficult choices we have to make when we find ourselves questioning the religion of our past in any capacity is deciding whether or not to go further. We eventually have to determine if what we are uncovering is enough, to keep going or stop digging, to choose just how much shaking we're willing to endure. Back then, I wasn't strong enough for that kind of turbulence. So I hid and hoped the shaking would pass. I know I'm not alone; I talk to shell-shocked believers every single day who are enduring their own theological tremors.

A year ago I received an e-mail from a pastor in Texas named Kyle, asking if we could speak. The suburban church plant he and his team had launched a little over a year before was growing quickly, so much so that they were already getting ready to start a huge building campaign and to create a permanent home for their community as they were outgrowing their current strip mall location. This should have been great news for Kyle, but he was exhausted and near burnout and close to tears. "I don't know what I believe about any of this anymore," he

told me, "and I don't know what to do or who I can talk to."
Over the past few months the questions he'd pushed beneath
the surface simply wouldn't stay buried anymore. His work
with the many LGBTQ Christians in his community had
blown up his preconceived ideas that Christian and gay were
mutually exclusive. This was a huge revelation and a tectonic
shift in his understanding of God. As a result he'd come to
reject the orthodox theology of sexual orientation, and this
conclusion had begun to disrupt everything. Like someone
stuck in a convenience store during an earthquake, stuff was
falling all around him and he was working breathlessly to keep
everything from crashing to the ground, all the while leading a
church and having to appear the very picture of blessed assur-
ance. The energy he expended every day to keep going through
the motions and acting as if his faith were stable and sturdy
was taking its toll on his marriage, his relationships, and his
physical health. Worst of all, his very identity as a pastor was
no longer secure, tied so tightly to a theology that needed to be
steady and a faith that was supposed to be unwavering. As we
talked, the panic in his voice was palpable and familiar. I know
that terror and the loneliness it yields. I've spent years ministering inside of it. I listened to Kyle and offered counsel, and I
wondered why so many religious communities like his—full of
good, loving, faithful people—end up making everyone afraid
to falter. I wondered what could be done to create an environment where a leader like Kyle could bring the full contents of
his heart out into the open, and how much more honestly he
could minister to his people.

And it isn't just pastors like Kyle who are carrying around
the incredible weight of losing their religion and trying to hide
it. Churches are packed with ordinary people who are trying
to keep it all together on the outside but falling quite apart
internally, feeling as though the bottom is dropping out for
good. It's not hard to see how this dissonance encourages hiding, especially among those who might cynically be called
"professional Christians." Pastors, ministers, and church staff
all learn rather quickly that doubts, theological deviations, and

faith crises feel like career liabilities. They are seen as signs of weakness, fatal flaws that hinder one's ability to minister and negatively impact the perception of those they serve. With this mind-set as the operating system, the most dangerous phrase a leader feels he or she can ever utter is "I don't know."

Yet this would be a welcome sound to the people who comprise the Church. It would be life-giving to the frustrated faithful trying to navigate the paradox of the spiritual journey, the tension of holding belief and doubt with equal vigor. What people in the seats and the pews so desperately desire are leaders who are willing to be vulnerable, who will give voice to the questions, who will give them permission to be unsure, who will make space at the table for their own vacillation. Instead, so many pastors choose a self-fulfilling prophecy in which they feel compelled to perpetuate the illusion of unwavering faith from the pulpit. They serve while burdened to present themselves to their congregations without blemish. Sadly, this incentive to hide ourselves trickles down to the larger church community, with everyone refraining from revealing their questions and conflicts for fear of being judged as inferior. People see the well-manicured facade of the flawless professionals on the platform and assume they must also be that sure in their faith in order to remain as part of the church family.

Jesus tells those who would follow after him that they would know a truth that would set them free (John 8:31–35), but so few Christians seem to have figured out what he was talking about or how to embrace this freedom. And herein lies the irony: the Church, both its leaders and congregations, keep ourselves in bondage, where the deepest recesses of our struggles and striving are never exposed, where we can never fully bring the weight of our questions to bear, never really knowing what our faith is made of. We discourage so much of the work that God is doing within each of us by never allowing it to reach the surface. Instead of finding affinity in our longings and questions, we each wrestle largely alone, never knowing that what we are experiencing is not only normal, but necessary, redemptive. In the process, everything of faith gets oversimplified. We turn the expansive, meandering experience of seeking and understanding the character of God and of living a life of response into some clear, all-or-nothing proposition where no gray or muddy areas are allowed.

I became complicit in this. I played the part of the unshakable pastor, despite the unrest in my spirit, despite my convictions that something was so very wrong regarding our treatment of the LGBTQ community. Regardless of the way I'd had so many lives around me testifying in opposition, I pushed down the questions like trash overflowing the bin, in order to buy me a little more time before dealing with it. My hope was that I'd either work through the internal conflicts and find some settling place for my soul, some uneasy truce with the holy discontent, or that I'd reach a place where I'd built up enough equity of trust in our community to become the first fully authentic pastor in history. I just needed a little more time. Many of us procrastinate away our spiritual renovation in this way. I didn't realize how toxic such a plan could become, just how treacherous a road it would be, how much time it would cause me to waste, how many people I neglected to care for well. The more and more entrenched I became in a church system I had great reservations about, the more beholden to it I became. As a result, tension steadily grew between who I was and who I was expected to be. I was being stretched further and further between my personal faith convictions and the amount of authenticity that I thought the community could bear.

I think that's why student ministry was the place I always felt most comfortable. Teenagers haven't quite learned the way you're "supposed" to do faith, and so they aren't overly concerned with conforming to an image of religiosity. They just want honest answers and honest questions, and they're far less likely to head screaming toward the hills (or worse, to the lead pastor's office) if you voice some divergence from orthodoxy, some deviation from the accepted party line. Teenagers' tables are usually far larger than their parents', as they've usually lived for their entire lives with more diversity and with fewer absolutes. This is often why younger people are critiqued harshly by religious people, but in my experience that openness has always resulted in something that better reflects the character of Jesus. Over time our student ministry became a space where the teenagers knew they were safe to expose the honest condition of their hearts, and in that environment we all thrived. It was the slow incubator for the pastor I would become and a small glimpse of the bigger table I longed to be part of building.

I learned a long time ago that the most God-honoring, most Jesus-reflecting act is to err on the side of loving people. When you simply accept those around you in whatever condition they come to you, the table naturally expands and relationship happens and God does stuff that you couldn't predict or control. This would become the character of our student ministry, and it would end up setting the tone for the larger church, pushing us outward and expanding our presence in the community and in the world. Some of my greatest ministry memories are from those times when emotionally exhausted teenagers would brave their fears of rejection enough to share with me the full contents of their hearts: those things about them that, based on their usual experience of church, they believed to be definite deal breakers. I saw at close range their utter relief when I let them know that no condemnation or expulsion was coming. It's a beautiful thing when the light goes on inside someone as they realize that they only need to be authentic and not perfect to be loved. This was something Jesus allowed people to see as he invited them to the table: their worth in the midst of their flaws. It's one of the most difficult lessons for people of faith to learn because we've been taught by the Church to believe the opposite. We've made it clear that believing the right things trumps everything else.

For the past two decades, I've tried to give people the gift of peace with their questions and their lack of surety, but for a long time I wasn't able to receive that gift myself—the grace to ask anything and to say everything. I hadn't yet summoned the courage to face the most terrifying questions Christians can ever ask themselves: "If this small part of my faith that I always believed to be true no longer is, what else might not be true?"

and "If the Bible doesn't say what I'd grown up believing it says in these handful of verses, where else have I gotten it wrong?" It begins to feel as though those questions themselves will destroy your faith for good, when in reality they should be welcome intrusions. Doubt isn't the sign of a dead faith, not necessarily even of a sickly one. It's often the sign of a faith that is allowing itself to be tested, one that is brave enough to see if it can hold up under stress. The worst thing you can do in those seasons of uncertainty is to pile upon your already burdened shoulders guilt for the mere fact that the wavering exists. God is more than big enough to withstand the weight of your vacillating belief, your part-time skepticism, and even your full-blown faith crises. We've been taught that such things are the antithesis of belief, usually by those who are afraid to be transparent about their own instability. God can handle your wavering, friend, even if those around you can't.

The pressure to be a pastor with flawless faith plagued me for a long decade and a half of pretending and denying and editing that really didn't help anyone. It just encouraged the hiding around me. I wish I had known then just how much freedom there is in sharing our doubts and questions, just how expansive the love of God is. I wish I had realized that I didn't need to choose or discard my whole religious history; that I didn't need to throw the baby Jesus out with the bathwater; that I could navigate a fully fleshed-out faith that didn't look like whatever I believed a *proper* one was supposed to look like. But I didn't. I was too entrenched in the thing, too fearful of the consequences of diverging, and too riddled with guilt to forge a new spiritual journey that made space for discovery and unknowns. I kept trying to maintain the facade and to compartmentalize my questions, but I could feel the tectonic plates of my religion colliding.

5

The Truth Shall Get You Fired

When deconstruction happens, many people simply abandon faith altogether, seeing it as some all-or-nothing proposition, believing that they need to completely sign off on a rigid list of doctrinal positions to be included. For me, deconstruction has been a relearning, seeing it all with new eyes. It's been a "born again" experience that has excavated God and helped me shed those things which are no longer helpful. The options are *not* either embracing the totality of the organized religion of your childhood or running into the arms of apostasy. Not surprisingly, that myth usually comes from organized religion; clearly defined, rigid systems are far easier to establish and maintain than the muddy, far more ambiguous process of sharing life together. On the contrary, there is an infinitely vast experience of Jesus, of the Bible, of the Holy Spirit, of Christian community that is available as we seek and discover together. So many people are beginning this journey in such a time as this, and often the only barrier to experiencing this rich spiritual renaissance is jettisoning the guilt that tells us this is all wrong, that it is a moral defect or character flaw.

It's easy for religious people to be intimidated by those seeking a bigger table. This was always the Pharisees' struggle. It wasn't lack of faith or lack of love for God, but a resistance to the idea that God could speak in new ways, could come packaged differently than they expected, and could exist outside of the box they built for God. When we dare to step outside of that box, when we ask the most difficult questions, and when we unearth our own spiritual junk, others are reminded of the unattended longing in their own hearts. Christian people rarely get angry at theological claims I make in my blog posts or when I'm speaking somewhere, but almost always at the questions I ask, because they are forced to entertain those questions themselves whether they care to or not. Those questions press against the tender spots where their doubt sits buried just below the surface.

The more I reflected on what I saw and experienced ten years earlier in Philadelphia and the more I began to dig into the clobber verses, the more I became certain that if I wanted to hold more tightly to Jesus, I was going to have to let go of a whole lot of cumbersome, damaging tradition. I was going to have to be a very different kind of pastor. At the time, I imagined that a change of environment would help in this transition, that I could start fresh somewhere and craft the church I could see in my head, and that somehow it would all be easier. This naive aspiration, as well as the deep grief over my father's sudden passing, clouded my vision when an opportunity came from a church three hours away in Raleigh, North Carolina. After some fierce internal wrestling and more than a few sleepless and tear-filled nights, we made the decision to leave our wonderful church in Charlotte after nearly a decade, anxious but excited to begin what we hoped would be the next long chapter in life and ministry. I believed the new community we were headed to wanted to do bold, audacious things to bring the love of Jesus to the city, and although we'd built up a comforting equity of trust in Charlotte and were well loved there, we let go of security and leaped toward the divine whisper.

We'd only been in our new home for a little over six months, however, when I heard God calling me to leave the church. I'd like to tell you that it was in my quiet time or in a dream or in a mellow, booming Morgan Freeman voice from the sky, but it was actually in the form of the senior pastor's voice saying, "You're fired," at a wobbly Starbucks table surrounded by a gawking audience of hipsters and housewives. God does indeed work in mysterious (and fairly embarrassing) ways. I'd felt the disconnection coming for a while (as you do in matters of career or love when you sense a relationship going sideways), but hearing the actual words scalded my heart just the same. I tried to hide the hurt with a poker face of detached cool, but I could feel my cheeks turning red and my pulse quickening.

"You don't fit here. You've never fit here," my pastor said matter-of-factly, as if trying to convince both of us that he was doing me a favor. (He was, of course, but it was hard to see that in the moment.) A small part of me was furious, but most of me agreed with him. I vacillated between wanting to tell him off and give him a bear hug. He was terribly wounding me, but he was right in ways he probably didn't realize. The truth was that I didn't fit and hadn't fit in a long time, at least not with this pastor and the church as he curated it. I had fit, however, with the people in the community, and with our students and families. I fit with the people I ministered to and served alongside. The ministry was growing and everything that I'd hoped to see happen when I arrived was beginning to happen. Our kids were slowly turning outward, the diversity of our group was growing, and excitement was building for us to leave the cloistered confines of our campus and to go express the counterintuitive love of God in the community in ways we'd never done before. Week by week we were starting to *become* the kingdom Jesus preached about, beginning to bring heaven down into our midst (Matt. 6:9–15). I felt like God was showing up daily and altering the proceedings and the people in beautiful ways: challenging us, stretching us, discomforting us. Just a day earlier, the spouse of one of my fellow pastors stopped me in the hallway at church and with great tenderness said, "You're exactly the person we need here." She shared how different things in our student ministry seemed now, how much God was doing, how fresh a breath it all seemed.

The reality was, though, that at the end of the day these things didn't really matter as much as I'd hoped they would. They weren't enough to keep me tethered there any longer. They didn't make me *fit*; not with this pastor, not in the cozy, carefully controlled system in place there, and not in the increasingly corporate experience I'd come to know as the American Church. Instead I began to feel like an outlier. I began to sense that there was a forceful current in place and that I was pushing hard against it. I hear that experience echoed by many church people as they embrace the full contents of their hearts and give loud voice to their faith crises, the struggle to find a secure place in the church community if they want to be fully known. It turns out religion actually manufactures misfits really well. It often creates such a narrow, rigid space for what a proper Christian is supposed to look like that many can't stay very long.

The Gospel writer Mark recalls a moment when Jesus is questioned as to why his students don't rigidly obey the laws of their faith tradition (Mark 2:18–22). Jesus' reply is telling: "No one sews a piece of unshrunk cloth on an old cloak; otherwise, the patch pulls away from it, the new from the old, and a worse tear is made. And no one puts new wine into old wineskins; otherwise, the wine will burst the skins, and the wine is lost, and so are the skins; but one puts new wine into fresh wineskins."

Jesus is telling his inquisitors and reminding us that responding to God will often push us to the boundaries of religion. It may cause tension. It may mean we outgrow the container we've been living in. If you feel like you don't fit, that might be really good news. A greater faith and bigger table may well be ahead, though you may have to tap-dance through a minefield on the way. You may have to endure adversity that doesn't feel at all worth it at the time. It certainly didn't feel that way when I was getting publicly fired in the coffee shop. Though this was the deepest wound yet, the truth is I'd begun accruing my scars decades earlier.

As with many people raised inside organized Christianity, I'd had a complicated relationship with it, and as the years went by the tension between us grew until it was tighter than a snare drum. Like many followers of Jesus, over time I'd learned to shelve the questions when they proved too difficult or uncomfortable or existentially messy. I ignored the nagging longings. I procrastinated away what I knew was going to be an invasive undertaking. Rather than expose it all, rather than risk the repercussions of complete revelation, I adapted through a regular cocktail of denial, silence, and fake-it-till-you-make-it religious busyness. I pretended all was well with my soul in hopes that I could prophesy it over myself and make it true.

On the outside, I had the productive, high-functioning superpastor thing down pat, yet I always carried this heavy holy unrest; feeling that the Church was supposed to be something, believing that it could be something, but so rarely seeing it materialize for more than a few fleeting days at a time. I saw brief flashes of beauty, but it never felt dangerous, only occasionally yielding to something bigger. It certainly never felt like the wild, unpredictable, unstoppable movement of the Spirit of God I read about in the New Testament, where people from every disparate corner of humanity came to find shared, interdependent, glorious purpose and stood in awe at the work of God in their midst. More often our local church simply felt like a successful midsize suburban company generating great faith-based entertainment every week. There were great facilities, nice people, folksy charm, and really well-produced, age-specific Sunday experiences—but the table was still smaller than it should have been, and it started to wear on me. The sustained pulling inside me was beginning to do damage. I was perpetually irritable. Community became laborious. Religion grew taxing.

Maybe you know what that's like. Maybe the difference between the Church you dream of and the one you're experiencing is taking its toll. Maybe you sense that something has to give, and you're just waiting for it all to hit the fan. Time is usually an impartial clarifier. The more it unfolds, the more you see, the more of reality you uncover whether or not you want to. For me, time was more like a fuse. As a pastor, the more burdened for the marginalized and the more outspoken I became, the greater dissonance I felt in the traditional church, and the more isolated I grew, the less joy I had pursuing God or serving God. I found the space I was expected to occupy as a card-carrying Christian pastor more and more ill fitting, ever more constraining, ever more toxic to my spirit. The chasm between my outer and inner selves widened as I tried to balance pastoral expectations and the actual condition of my heart. The less honest I could be, the more energy and time I had to spend on perception management, the more maintenance my outward spirituality required. When that happens in us, when the duplicity within us becomes too great, we soon discover the cracks getting bigger, and we eventually find ourselves in faith crisis. For me, something had to give, and there in that coffee shop, amid the hiss of foam machines and the mingling chatter of strangers, something did.

I didn't realize it then, but that was the beginning of my emancipation from organized American Christianity. It was the breaking of a critical chain that I would have never broken on my own. This terrible moment wasn't a landing pad but a launching pad, a spectacular gift wrapped in apparent disaster. Had I known it then, I would have danced out the door. Instead I called my wife and told her not to unpack any more boxes, and I had a good cry as I mourned this particular dream. I didn't even get a coffee for the road—I hate coffee.

The following Sunday I found myself in cold, unfamiliar waters. That morning I woke up for the first time in seventeen years without a local community to care for, without a building to head toward, without measurable "ministry" to do. It was a decided feeling of existential homelessness. I had no job, no plan, and no idea what Sunday mornings were supposed to look like now. I did have plenty of *other* things though: questions about where the road was leading from here, pragmatic worries like a mortgage and loss of income and my kid's feet (which seemed to be outgrowing shoes daily). I also had a wild,

unruly assortment of insecurities, doubts, and fears all competing loudly for my time. Thankfully I now had plenty to spare
and could entertain them all—at least for a couple of hours.

Later that day I took a good look at my family across the
table from me and decided that I needed to finish the funeral
for my past and start looking for the life again. I decided that
I could either wallow in the rejection and hopelessness which
really wanted to have their way with me, or I could do what I'd
been doing since this faith journey began: trusting that God
is, that God is good, and that loving people will lead me to
where I need to be without knowing it. I started to rest in these
things in a way I hadn't had to in a while. And instead of seeing the moment with dread, I chose to look with expectancy.
I saw the gifts I'd been given. For the first time in fifteen years
I wasn't burdened with a set of pastoral expectations. I wasn't
responsible to a community. I didn't need to toe a company
line. I didn't have to represent anyone's faith but my own. I
could watch football and have lunch with my family and not
shower. I could be every bit the vacillating, doubting, hurting,
frustrated soul I was without apology. I could be more honest
than I'd ever been about what I believe and don't believe and
be OK with all of it again. Unfettered by the annoying entan-
glements of a salary, health insurance, or gainful employment,
I could decide whether or not I still wanted to be a pastor, if
I still considered myself a Christian, and if the Church was a
place I ever wanted to return to.

Over the course of the next few hours and days, gravity
began to loosen its grip on my spirit. I started to feel lighter. I
began to feel less like I was falling and more like I was flying.
My wife would later say, "Getting fired was the greatest thing
that ever happened to you." I wasn't at all ready to say that just
yet, but hope was rising up. I was learning to trust God again.

This is so many people's faith story: that realization that once
you've gotten some space between yourself and the Church, the
landscape becomes wider, you feel untethered. For some the
road away from organized religion leads them smack-dab into
Jesus, though not without a great deal of heartache. For the

past three years I've walked people through their own apparent disasters looking for hope, searching for the voice of God in the wreckage of their spiritual journeys. It's bloody, brutal work, but it's some of the most sacred ground I've stepped upon.

Not long ago I received an e-mail from a young youth pastor named Trent, whose story is so very familiar. He's serving at a large church in the heart of the Bible Belt. His once-secure theology has gradually begun to shift, and he's been struggling with feeling compelled to speak but terrified into silence. The tension has manifested itself in lots of misplaced anger, and his family and marriage have all been impacted by the unrest in him. Ministry has become a pollutant, and he is shaken. I replied to him, shared some of what I'd been learning, and talked practically about how he could begin to walk this out, but in the back of my mind I wondered if this advice would do the trick. I was praying for a breakthrough for Trent because I knew what a tough spot he was in. A small part of me wished for his firing.

When the conflicts in our spiritual journey become too profound, something eventually has to give if we want to find the place of peace and rest the writer of the Twenty-third Psalm speaks of. There is often a steep price to pay to be the most authentic version of ourselves. The prophets and the disciples and the early Christians understood this, but we've been conditioned to believe we can have our religious convictions with little or no alteration to our daily existence. But the truth is, real spirituality is usually costly. Many followers of Jesus end up learning this not from the world *outside* the Church but from our faith tradition itself. We end up choosing Jesus and losing our religion; finding proximity to him creates distance from others. If you seek to expand the table, you're going to find yourself in a tough spot. The truth may not get you fired. (Although it might.) It may just make you the odd man out at Thanksgiving dinner, it might cause a schism in your small group, it could bring turbulence to your marriage, it might fracture your friendships. But so often, these traumatic breaks allow you the necessary time and space to breathe, to see the wide expanse laid out in front of you, and to listen again for the voice of God and to run (or at least limp) toward it. These relational and career tragedies give gifts that we could receive no other way. That tiny coffee-shop table was the scene of a deep and profound wounding, and in the moment it beat the hell out of me—but it was also a holy space. It was the pivot point, the place where my plot was twisting. It was liftoff.

PART TWO

Building the Bigger Table

6
Jesus the Table Setter

I grew up in a fairly typical Italian family, in which one's house is really just an expensive, elaborate covering for the kitchen. *That* was where we lived. That was the hub of life. There at the kitchen table, we talked and laughed and told stories. We caught up with each other and we gossiped and we argued and we entertained—and we ate and ate and ate. The kitchen was the place where, over a million seemingly ordinary moments, our family became a family. In reality, it turns out, there are no such things as ordinary days, and Jesus' life and ministry testify to this. When he tells his closest friends over a last meal to remember him whenever they gather around the table together (Luke 22:7–23), he is inviting them to notice the holy in the mundane, to acknowledge his presence in the unremarkable, to make acknowledging him part of the normal rhythm of life. This is perhaps the greatest challenge we experience along the spiritual journey: remembering. But if we begin to ascribe meaning to even the most commonplace moments, we can create a life saturated with an awareness of the Divine.

As eventful as the ordinary days could be in our home, holidays were uniquely special because on those days we outgrew the kitchen table and graduated to the dining room table. New faces appeared and new voices filled the air; introductions and reconnections were made. And when the gatherings were especially large, actual construction would be required. My father would retrieve two massive rectangular pieces of wood from the garage, and after removing half a year's dust from them, we would all pull the table from either end, and it would magically slide open and we'd drop those slabs in and add more chairs. We quite literally expanded the table so that we could fit everyone. We made room we didn't have before. This was a regular incarnation of the love of God right in the center of our home, though we never knew to name it as such. This is the heart of the gospel: the ever-expanding hospitality of God. Jesus, after all, was a carpenter. Building bigger tables was right in his wheelhouse.

What struck me when I began to read the Gospel stories was Jesus' *table ministry*, the way he so often used the act of sharing a meal, the act of breaking bread, as a way of letting people know that they were seen and heard and known and respected. With great regularity Jesus used the common moments to incubate the sacred—everything becoming a sort of a living parable to illustrate the tangible reality of spirituality. The table was an altar around which he welcomed the world to experience communion with God and with one another. We easily forget that faith is a relational experience, that it is almost impossible to move into Christlikeness without other souls to extend compassion and mercy and love to, or to receive those things from. And so while the introvert in me loves when Jesus retreats to the solitary places to pray, he doesn't stay there long, soon moving toward humanity to pour out those things poured into him in private. Most startling was the diversity of Jesus' table. He gathered with priests and prostitutes, with the religious elite and the common street rabble, with his disciples and with his adversaries. (How many of us can say we willingly gather with those who dislike or oppose or displease us, that we seek fellowship with those whom we perceive to be our enemies?) There at the big table they were all treated with equal dignity, and they all left his presence with that dignity intact—even if he sometimes had hard words for them.

In the times of Jesus even more so than today, the act of sharing a meal with someone was a sign of respect, of association with another—of one's willingness to be seen in fellowship. It was a very public endorsement. Because of this, Jesus' diverse choice of meal companions often made people really angry. The religious folks are quoted several times in the Scriptures saying, "Look at him! This man eats with sinners!" (for example, Luke 15:1–7). They wonder aloud what kind of proper rabbi would associate himself with such reprehensible characters, and they seek to undermine his authority because of his proximity to those on the margins. Then as now, we're often known by the company that we keep, especially in the Church, and Jesus wasn't helping his rep with the religious elites. While we don't see it specifically mentioned in the text, I imagine the street people often criticized him for breaking bread with the Pharisees too, accusing him of conspiring with their oppressors or contributing to their marginalization. This is the specific tension we are called to live in as we seek to create conversation where there has been silence, as we try to forge relationship where there has been estrangement. When we look to expand the table, we will invariably be pulled in all directions by those who are more interested in claiming ownership of our allegiance than extending grace to the other. The more I've sought to be about the work of loving all people, the more I've come to see how that will really piss off *some* people. Jesus didn't meet with just those who were deemed his social equals or those who could further his cause or those who would boost his platform. (In fact, he specifically warns against such self-serving hospitality; see Luke 14:12–14.) He had friends in low places too. That was the strategic beauty of his scandalously diverse guest list. By not being selective with his invitation, Jesus affirms the value of his disparate meal companions to them *and* to those watching from a distance.

In a world where we so often are content to preach only to the choirs of those who agree with us, to wall ourselves off in a social-media echo chamber of our amen-ing cheerleaders, Jesus models a better way. He fully engages all sides and teaches them about one another in the process. For him the table is a tool of connection. It transcends difference. It bridges disagreement. It declares the other welcomed and worthy of hearing. It recognizes the other and declares commonality with him or her. I don't see very much of this in the modern Christian expression here in America. I don't know if we're really all that interested in proximity with those who differ from us. I'm not sure we care to follow Jesus all the way to the table with those we have contempt for from a distance, and yet this is the path of the disciple. In Matthew 5:9, Jesus says that those wishing to reflect the character of God must be "makers of peace." At the center of this was the idea of creating *shalom* for others, enabling them to have the same access to wholeness, sustenance, justice, and joy as anyone else. It was not merely some internal understanding about the intrinsic value of all people he held in his heart, but the tangible, visible response in the world that affirmed this understanding whenever that value was disregarded. And invariably this making of peace will need to be extended to those whose religious beliefs, politics, and behavior don't seem to be compatible with our own. We will be required to reach beyond our preferences and comfort. No matter how inclusive or open we imagine our hearts to be, Jesus will always cause us to stretch further than we are comfortable with, always seeking greater diversity, more justice, deeper renovation.

This means that we endure the tension of creating peace for another while experiencing discomfort ourselves. It also means that expanding the table isn't just about entitled conservatives needing to make room for marginalized communities or progressive Christians; it's also about those whose religious convictions are far left of center finding a way to continually seek understanding *of* and to extend invitation *to* those who may stand in complete opposition to them. The bigger table cannot be for ourselves and only those who are to the left *or* the right of us. Redemptive community requires that we extend the invitation to both sides of our political and religious perspectives, and endeavor to build relationship, or at the very least under-standing. This is perhaps the greatest challenge Jesus provides us with; it is the counterintuitive compassion we are asked to cultivate. The 2016 presidential election and the decades-long politicizing of the Church have made bridging such expanses more challenging than it's ever been.

One of the most powerful examples of Jesus' table ministry is recorded by all four of the Gospel biographies.* Jesus has been teaching in a remote spot and the place is packed. It's getting late and those gathered, miles away from the nearest Chick-fil-A, are getting hungry. Jesus, drawn to the need by his disciples, responds by feeding the whole lot of them with the small bit of food present. As the story goes, thousands have their bellies filled and some get to-go boxes. As so often hap-pens when reading these stories, we can easily be tripped up by the miraculous aspect of the moment, preoccupied by the mechanism rather than the meaning of it all. If we see this meal as merely a *how story*, we will be forever burdened with intel-lectually explaining the exponential multiplication of the bread and fish, trying to wrap our minds around the physics and food science involved—and we will be doomed to miss the point gloriously. But if we view this as a *who story* and a *why story*, we will find the clear invitation for we who seek the ways of Jesus. We can see the heart of God for hungry people. We can see the tremendous challenge of expanding the table. *This* is where the miracle takes place.

I can't fathom the transformation of a basket of food to accommodate a multitude (heck, I'm not even sure how our toaster works), but I can see the boundless compassion of the open table and endeavor to re-create that on whatever spot I stand at any given moment and with the people in my midst. Jesus feeds people. That's what he does. And as striking as what he does is, equally revelatory is what he *doesn't* do here. There's

*The books of Matthew, Mark, Luke, and John, known as the Gospels, are four separate books claiming to be accounts of Jesus' life by the disciples bearing their names. Thus, I prefer to refer to them as biographies.

no altar call, no spiritual gifts assessment, no membership class, no moral screening, no litmus test to verify everyone's theology and to identify those worthy enough to earn a seat at the table. Their hunger and Jesus' love for them alone, nothing else, make them worthy. This is a serious gut check for us.

Invariably we will be required to dispense compassion and mercy upon those we deem undeserving of it. We will be challenged to extend love to people we may find quite unlovable. We will be called to care for the "least of these," who are so not because society disregards them—but often because we in the church have. Sadly, in areas of racial equality, LGBTQ rights, ethnic diversity, and gender equality, the Church has been on the tail end of progress, hindered by its tradition. For as much as we claim to take our cue from Jesus, we've so frequently resisted the progressive, barrier-breaking heart of his ministry. To love the least in *his* likeness will involve repairing a great deal of the damage organized Christianity has done to historically marginalized communities, and in many cases, we'll need to push back in opposition to it from the inside.

I was recently at an interfaith gathering, talking to a woman about the difficulties she's experienced as a Christian married to a Jewish man. She told me the story of looking for the common ground with her in-laws and of the surprising revelation her husband's mother shared with her one afternoon. "I've been thinking a lot about chicken soup," she said. "No matter where you travel to on the planet, nearly everyone eats chicken soup in some form or another. It might have this spice or that spice, it might be served with rice or noodles or dumplings or matzo balls—but it's basically still chicken soup." She looked at her daughter-in-law and said, "Maybe God is *there*. Maybe, if we can come together and share chicken soup and keep talking, then maybe there's a way forward."

Friend, this is what it means to be the people of the bigger table: to look for the threads that might tie us together and to believe that these are more powerful than we imagine. This is the only future the Church really has. Disparate people will not be brought together through a denomination or a pastor or by anything the institutional church can offer. We know that now. These were useful for a time, but they are an exercise in diminishing returns. The Church will thrive only to the degree it is willing to be about making space for a greater swath of humanity and by recognizing the redemptive power of real relationships.

As a young Christian I assumed that the more you learned about Jesus and the more you sought to emulate him, the more your table would naturally expand. I thought that the more you lived in the image of Christ, the greater your hospitality for the world would become and the more diverse your community would be. I believed that if you still had condition and caveat on your hospitality, if you still had a selective invitation, then you were not quite yet fully saturated with the love of God. I believed that a church most in the image of Jesus would have the biggest table on the planet—and then I started serving in the Church. Maybe you've experienced the same deflating disconnect of not finding Jesus in the institution that bears his name, of wanting something bigger than the religion you've inherited.

The good news is that you're not alone. You are one of hundreds of millions of faithful but frustrated orphans looking for home. The even better news is that the way there is a whole lot simpler than we've imagined it to be. Jesus models the better way. He sets the bigger table. We don't have to reinvent Church or create a new system or launch a new denomination. We don't need a ministry strategy or a building campaign or some magic words. We simply follow him to the table of our own hospitality. We pull that sucker open, drop in a couple extra slabs of wood, and start adding chairs. This is how we become a family. This is how we find our place and set one for others. It's how we make chicken soup for the world.

Expanding the table isn't about digging in our heels around religious rules, doctrine, or dogma. Those things will always provide us reason to disconnect from others. They will always become obstacles. No, this is about the mind-set with which we gather with people, about creating a space where the differences can be both openly acknowledged and fully welcomed.

The four "legs" of the bigger table we'll talk about in the coming chapters are the core values, the nonnegotiables that are needed regardless of our theological leanings, political affiliations, or personal convictions. They are the places where we will need to do the most invasive internal work if we are to create truly redemptive community where everyone can be fed.

7

Radical Hospitality

Have you ever been a guest in someone's house where they absolutely spoiled you to the point that you wanted to live there? (Grandparents are masters at this, if my kids are any indication.) Not long ago I stayed at the home of a new friend while on a West Coast speaking trip. After a wonderfully warm greeting at the airport and a stop for a delicious lunch punctuated with laughter and great stories, we headed to their home. The house itself was an absolute stunner, perched high on a hilltop overlooking miles of rolling California wine country, with floor-to-ceiling glass doors facing the brilliant panorama below. It was like stepping into a living impressionist landscape painting, one that changed color by the hour. But the house and the view, as beautiful as they were, weren't the star of my stay. The warmth of the family's welcome was. My room was stocked with books and things to make me feel comfortable, my favorite everyday foods were already in the pantry, and a personal card on the bedside table reiterated that while I was there, I was family. My hosts' manner of care, their consideration of my needs, and their effusive affection let me know that my presence mattered and that my arrival was anticipated.

Because of this I was able to feel at home in a place I'd never been before, which itself is a small miracle. A few minutes later I sprawled in an oversized lounge chair and heard myself exhaling loudly. Many of us so rarely get to really breathe anymore, especially in the Church.

We can usually tell when we're being received with great joy and when we're greeted with ambivalence, if we're being celebrated or merely being tolerated—and the two can be equally transformative. The reception we receive in someone's presence can determine whether or not we stay or if we ever come back. This is true of people we encounter, businesses we patronize, groups we join. If we're made to feel like an unwanted inconvenience anywhere, we're rarely anxious to return. Turns out, ambivalence isn't all that attractive, is it? This is a fairly universal truth. Why it's so difficult for religious institutions to figure this out is anyone's guess, but many of us have found ourselves feeling like barely endured houseguests in faith communities for any number of reasons: our appearance, skin color, gender identity, sexual orientation, theology. We know well the silent uneasiness of realizing that though we are physically present, emotionally we are being kept at a distance—that our inclusion is highly provisional and only begrudgingly accepted. This is what *tolerance* feels like, and why it's one of the most useless ideas in our efforts to expand the table of the Church's hospitality. Tenuous, halfhearted coexistence isn't a worthy aspiration for we who claim to follow or emulate Jesus, though that seems to be what far too many churches believe the goal to be. Christ calls his disciples to love one another, not to tolerate one another, and not as we imagine that to look, or the way we construct the concept around our fear and biases—but out of the sum total of his life and ministry. If reluctantly putting up with people is the bar we've set in the Church, we're hardly imitating Jesus, and we're going to continue creating a table far too small for the name we claim.

In the thirteenth chapter of John's Gospel biography, the writer shares a revelatory moment that speaks to the hospitable heart of Jesus (13:1–17). Gathering for one of the final times with his students and closest friends, he rises from the table, wraps a towel around his waist, assumes a servant's posture, and begins to wash their (likely filthy) feet. Such a gesture of humility was unexpected and well below his social standing, as is reflected in his student Peter's incredulity at the very idea. The writer takes note that in attendance at the meal is Judas Iscariot, the disciple who would soon betray Jesus and precipitate his arrest, beating—and execution. This makes Jesus' act of service all the more radical in its counterintuitive kindness; he extends hospitality to one who had essentially become his enemy. The gesture is a living parable for us, a reminder that we are to be the *washers of feet*, not only for those whom we deem worthy or with whom we have affinity, but also for those we are offended by, angered by, or disagree with—those we are least inclined to welcome. It means that whatever caveat we would add as a condition to welcoming or serving another (race, sexual orientation, gender, political affiliation) will need to be removed. This kind of lavish acceptance is something people are craving but experiencing less and less in the Church these days, and they're rightly going elsewhere for it.

Jesus' kind of hospitality is transformative for both the guest and the host. A few years ago I traveled to an orphanage in Nairobi, Kenya. Most of the children there were rescued from one of the massive slums nearby, miles and miles of interconnected makeshift structures built precariously from pieces of wood and oddly shaped scraps of metal, with no plumbing and only random twisted snakes of wires providing a bit of spotty and dangerous electricity. When we arrived at the center, the children greeted our arrival with an almost embarrassingly exuberant reception, treating us with an openhanded kindness that I've rarely experienced. Dressed in their absolute best, they danced and sang and embraced us and gave us pictures they had drawn, with words of love and appreciation crafted before we'd spent a second there. They celebrated us more than anyone has ever celebrated them. I felt the hot, dark chocolate ground beneath me and knew it was holy. I was meeting Jesus. My eyes kept filling with tears I tried hard to fight back. It would soon become impossible. On our first day we took a tour of the facility and visited the children's sleeping area. It was a large, open, nondescript cinder-block room with high ceilings, lined with rows of simple, unadorned wooden bunk beds, a small box beside each of them containing a child's sole material possessions. These consisted of a few sets of clothes, some stationery, and a small toy or stuffed animal. As I passed one of the bunks, I noticed words carved into its headboard. I leaned in to get a closer look. It said: "This is my bed and I love it." *These* were our hosts, the ones welcoming and spoiling us. These were the battered souls lavishing kindness upon us. Out of their very meager resources, they'd made overflow. They, like Jesus feeding the crowds, multiplied their *little*, so that it became an abundance that they shared with us.

There's a counterintuitive humility that comes when we are treated with such regard at the table. Rather than being inflated into arrogance or becoming bloated with self-importance, we actually find ourselves shrinking to our proper proportions. We feel simultaneously small *and* grateful. And that's really the beauty of radical hospitality, the way it right-sizes us, the way it strips away our ego and simply ascribes value to us and allows us to find comfort in that knowledge. When we are fully welcomed, we are able to rest in the presence of others, not needing to earn or achieve or do or make anything. When we no longer feel compelled to prove our worth, we can simply fall into our belovedness—and we exhale.

The Church begins to expand the table by providing the kind of hospitality that equally embraces everyone, not pulling some close and keeping others at a distance. This must happen in our faith communities from both a telescopic and a microscopic view. It must be explicitly expressed from the pulpit and in the language of our mission statements and promotional material. It needs to be printed and spoken and taught and repeated and modeled by ministers to those in the pews, and it has to be something imprinted on our individual hearts: our personal relentless pursuit of the welcome of Jesus for everyone, even those we find most difficult to welcome.

When I was a young boy growing up in the 1980s, I remember hearing how New York City mayor Ed Koch used to travel around town and ask any constituents he ran into, whether they were Wall Street tycoons, Harlem cab drivers, or Upper East Side housewives, the same simple question: "How'm I doin'?" And then he would look them in the eyes and listen to their concerns about the way the city was being run. I imagine the responses he received weren't always pleasant, but I bet he heard what he sometimes needed to hear. I imagine that he left those exchanges different than before, and I'm quite sure the people speaking with him did too. This happens whenever we feel seen and heard.

The Church tends to do a whole lot of speaking and a whole lot less listening these days. Things began changing for me as a pastor and a person of faith when I began to see ministry more as sitting with people and listening to their stories, rather than standing at a distance and trying to dazzle them with brilliant words. That simple act of sharing space with people is a sacred offering, and in a world where most of us are content to shout our opinions at relative strangers from a safe space, the radical hospitality of Christ pulls people closer and demands that we see and hear them. And once we view a person in the illuminating light of actual relationship, we can't help but see the God in them; we feel the presence of the Divine; we welcome Jesus into our midst as we meet with them. And when we do taste the redemptive fruit of truly knowing a person, we will never settle for less than that again.

Every single church in the world is a friendly church. Just ask their pastors. Better yet, scan their Web sites, their Sunday bulletins, or their promotional videos, and you can be sure that the description includes something about being warm and welcoming, about being known as "the friendly church," about all people being able to come as they are, no matter what. They all promise a wide, fully open door; all fancy their campuses as loving, hospitable environments for everyone—even if the evidence is sometimes less than convincing. It's as if they say it once somewhere in their genesis as young church plants and then simply believe it to be so moving forward, rarely reassessing the claim again. They simply assume that they are reflecting the heart of Jesus accurately to disparate groups of people. Church leaders and their communities rarely want to dig any deeper, to look closer, to believe that they may be cold and distant to visitors, that they might in actuality be highly selective in their welcome, or that many people, for a variety of reasons, do not feel as though they can come as *they* are.

That's largely because more and more churches are wired and built to bring people in the front door, with very few concerns about who is leaving out the back door. This has quickly become the standard, go-to template for creating a vibrant, millennial-attracting church: create an appealing Sunday worship experience, around which all the bells and whistles of welcome teams and children's ministries and lobby amenities are carefully placed. These all give the believable appearance of hospitality, but often this is only a surface veneer. It tends to provide the illusion of welcome, yet peer beneath that thin facade to see the reception many receive, and it's no surprise that these folks quickly sense the distance and soon vanish from the community without much fanfare or grieving. And yet it is those very people, whom organized Christianity is often failing the greatest, whom we are most in need of listening to because they expose our gradually acquired blind spots and allow us to recover the purity of our faith tradition.

I now spend a great part of my days with these folks: hearing their stories, listening to their heartbreak, and trying to create spiritual community in direct response to it all. So few churches have the emotional bandwidth, the time, or the desire to do this work because it is a momentum killer and an agenda changer. It disrupts the plan. Imagine if churches met as frequently to discuss the diversity of their congregations or to reach out to those who have disappeared as they do for their Sunday service planning or building campaigns. What if, rather than perfecting and spit-shining our worship gatherings and stocking our coffee bars, we made seeing and hearing people our priority? What if, instead of the church experience being a room where one person talks and a few folks sing for an hour to rows of people in chairs, we figuratively and quite literally set the table for people to gather, to be uncomfortable, to see people and linger long enough to recognize the Divine within themselves and others? What if pastors and churches, instead of preparing faith-based entertainment, simply existed to set the table? What if our church staffs, instead of functioning as professional Christians there to upload content, became gracious, loving hosts? Spending more time putting our collective heads together and figuring out how our church communities can begin concretely reflecting the radical hospitality of Jesus would be transformative. It would call us to reconfigure our ministries and rearrange the way we spend money and craft content and train people. Most importantly, it would bring the kind of revolution that no clever sermon series or creative outreach ever could. This would be something that sticks.

And yet as rare as it is when a church engages in this invaluable kind of introspection, we do it with even less frequency in our own homes and families and in our personal interactions with people. We simply assume that because we love Jesus, we are loving others like Jesus does; that because we feel at home with him, people feel that way in our presence. We take for granted that our table is God-sized or rationalize away why that may not be true. Few of us stop to consider whom we're excluding or whom we're reluctant to welcome or how we've become a barrier to other people, because this kind of self-awareness and self-examination is fraught with land mines. We're forced to do some work and consider our own darkness. It's one thing to personally accept Christ's boundless grace, and another to avoid hoarding it for ourselves. It's always so much easier to live with a closed fist than an open hand. And yet, the latter is the way of Christ. This is the heart of his hospitality. This should be our daily bread—and it will cause us to move.

There's a popular progressive Christian myth that says if Jesus were here today, he would be hanging out solely with the poor and the disenfranchised and the outcasts. This is not

entirely true, if the Gospel biographies are to be believed anyway. They show him giving equal time to the most disparate
segments of humanity. He isn't (as so many Christians tend to
be) cloistered in some cozy, insulated corner, preaching to the
choir of his like-minded fan club, but he also isn't relegated
to the ragged, gritty, neglected people of the street either. Yes,
he dines with sinners and tax collectors, but also in the home
of a respected Pharisee, surrounded by the skeptical religious
elites. He extends his hand to heal a despised leper, but does
the same for the servant of an occupation Roman soldier whose
faith moves him. He preaches on a hillside to the poor and
disenfranchised, yet regularly speaks in the synagogues amid
the experts and insiders. He counsels both a curious Pharisee
named Nicodemus who comes to him under the cover of night
and a shunned Samaritan woman at a public well in the heat of
the day (Luke 7:36; 7:1–10; 4:44; John 3:1–21; 4:1–30). Jesus
was a shepherd, a pastor to the wide swath of humanity that
crossed his path, caring for all of these people with the same
fervency and reverence. Even the Pharisees and Sadducees, the
Jewish religious elite for whom he saved his most pointed criti-
cisms, received his presence and welcome. And this is perhaps
one of the most challenging things we face as we seek to personally emulate him: equally embracing those we find unpleas-
ant or unlovable or unworthy of welcome. We all have (as U2
singer Bono calls them) "lepers in our heads," those we keep at
a distance, people we would rather not see seated at our table,
those we elevate ourselves above.

Hospitality ascribes value to people. It declares them worth
welcoming. It disarms them by easing the fears that past rejection has yielded and lets them know that this place is different.
And once people realize that they are received with joy, they
begin to rest in it. They breathe again. I talk to so many people
who never feel such comfort in the Church, and this is perhaps
one of our greatest shared sins: through omission or excuse or
refusal, we are inhospitable places to people. Jesus' openness
was seen by many as a liability, perhaps because it was simply
threatening to their neatly delineated morality codes. It created

tension then, and it will do the same as we replicate it. Radical hospitality will always transcend the existing constructs, always reach beyond current boundaries, always put stress on the system in place. This is why Jesus' meals with "sinners" were so disconcerting to the religious folks: they could sense that things were shifting, and that they would need to shift too. And when Jesus says, "The tax collectors and the prostitutes are going into the kingdom of God ahead of you" (Matt. 21:31), he is telling the elitists that they are missing what he is doing, that the table is expanding despite them, and that they'd better make room in their community and in their hearts. Because they were so unwilling to welcome those they believed to be inferior to them, they never saw Jesus fully in their midst. Whenever marginalized groups find welcome, those with the power and position will always feel they are losing something, and they will cling tightly to a privilege that feels like it's evaporating.

This fearful mind-set was fully exploited by Donald Trump and was undoubtedly central to his election. White people were given and believed the narrative that they were persecuted, that they were threatened, that their decline was imminent—despite every advantage still being afforded them. Diversity and equality will often be interpreted as attack by the privileged, and they will fight to prevent the presence of both. One of the most Jesus-replicating acts we can engage in is confronting our blind spots of privilege. This lack of self-awareness was true of the Pharisees and Sadducees, and it's true of those who've had the run of the Church in our recent history. These will be the people who fight to keep the table smaller.

This is the turbulence that radical hospitality creates. It will continually make room for those who are not yet represented and not yet welcomed, and it will force those of us already comfortably ensconced to discard some of our biases and fears and securities to do so. When we receive someone in a way that incarnates Jesus, our desire to see and hear and know them becomes greater than our desire to be comfortable. In this way we grow in Christlikeness to the degree that we are willing to be inconvenienced by the needs of others. This selflessness is a marker of our personal proximity to Jesus—and it's as elusive as it is sacred. Radical hospitality disregards the pushback it might get for welcoming those not currently included; it occurs when another's sense of belonging trumps the cost of demanding their inclusion. It begins to sustain wounds on behalf of the wounded. It finds kinship with the hurting. It manufactures activists and allies, because it recognizes that we are all interdependent and that until all are welcomed with the same vigor, the Church is less in the image of God than it could and should be. This is the place where the table of Jesus is set, and it is where we find Christ in the eyes of another.

8

Total Authenticity

The Gospel writer Mark recounts the story of a desperate man who brings his gravely ill son to Jesus in the hopes that Jesus will heal him (9:14–29). The author doesn't tell us about the man's theology or his religious history, just that when he is faced with the question of whether or not Jesus is the real deal and can do this miraculous work, the man says: "I believe; help my unbelief!" I get *that* guy. Now *that guy* I understand. This is the spiritual journey for most of us, if we're honest enough to admit it. We all spend a great deal of our time in that seemingly oxymoronic tension of simultaneously holding faith and doubt in concert. We all vacillate wildly between certainty and disbelief, often many times in the same day. The difference between us and the father in this story is that he has the stones to say it. He isn't too worried or proud to admit the full contents of his heart. I want to be like him when I grow up.

The truth is that all pastors lie. They usually don't initially intend to, they just often come to realize that they need to—that their livelihoods may depend on it. I began ministry just a normal, flawed guy who was perfectly fine admitting it. Over time, though, I gradually crafted a renovated, sanitized version of myself suited for public consumption in my church, and with it the table of my hospitality in a very practical way began to shrink. I can remember the day I realized a group of my students had grabbed my iPhone and being terrified they'd see my iTunes playlist and how much Prince and AC/DC was on it. I wanted them to think I was the pastor I thought I was *supposed* to be. But this ran much deeper than just the music I listened to. I also distanced myself from people who would disrupt the carefully crafted facade of religiosity I'd cultivated: people with jagged edges, messy folks, non-Christians. The deeper I walked into spiritual leadership, the more comfortable with this pretending I became, until I finally lost the ability to discern what was me and what was my religious costume. One day I turned around and didn't recognize myself. I began to grieve the smallness of life, the lack of diversity around me. Not only was I now surrounded solely by other Christians, but only by other Christians from my church, and only those who I easily clicked with. My table had gotten staggeringly small, and what's more, I didn't feel all that comfortable sitting at it. I began to miss the wide-open spaces of my life back in Philadelphia, where people weren't souls to save or projects to take on, where judgment wasn't my default response. More than that, I really grieved the honest version of myself that I'd lost as I became entrenched in my Christianity. I was homesick for *me*.

This blurriness of self is more common to those in the Church than I realized then. At the time, I felt like the lone actor in a massive sea of real people, and it was a precarious place to live and minister from. Now, I speak to so many current or former ministers and church staff members who are stuck in this very same identity crisis, this same existence of pretending, this same sadness. They desperately want authenticity but are terrified because they believe this is no longer possible for them—the consequences are simply too great.

But this isn't true of professional Christians alone. Whether in matters of theology or sexuality or in our interaction with the world, we often soften or altogether conceal the truest parts of ourselves to keep in good standing with our peers. If we're not careful and continually fighting against it, organized religion has a way of making us all chronically insincere. We come to conclude that we can't be fully ourselves; we can only be the heavily edited, carefully censored, highly selective versions of ourselves that we believe will allow us to stay comfortably in the community. And this is one of our most treacherous fault lines of organized Christianity. Though the Church is supposed to be a "come as you are" gathering, we realize soon after arriving that for any number of reasons, we can't really come as *we* are. Over time we all learn how to continually *read the room* to determine the exact parameters of our personal mess that we can reveal without alienating ourselves. We begin to craft a Church-specific self, and life becomes about perception management more than open and true pursuit of God. Though full authenticity in our faith communities should be invited and celebrated, in reality it's often a terrible liability. "Say it all," we think to ourselves, "and our days here are numbered." This is perhaps the most common response people give me for no longer being connected to a local church: because somewhere along the way, some part of their personal revelation proved too much for those they were in community with and they were met with devastating distance and silence. And these forced prodigals should all be welcomed home by the expression of Jesus the Church is called to be.

Sandra introduced herself as an *ex-minister* in her first e-mail to me about a year ago, and as is true with thousands of people I speak to each year, I quickly learned that her exile was not self-induced or welcomed. After fourteen years of faithful, productive ministry in her Kentucky town, retirement was chosen for her by those in her faith community who'd grown more and more uncomfortable with the honesty she brought to the Sunday pulpit. Regularly admitting her moments of internal doubt and her private wrestling with certain passages of Scripture with her congregation, Sandra had been faced with a terrible and all-too-common choice by the power holders who defined the parameters of the table: stop sharing so much or be removed. For Sandra there was no decision to be made. She told me, "I'd rather be an honest ex-minister than an employed liar." A few months later, she was relieved of her position. Though heartbroken, she is now doing what so many find themselves doing: crafting ministry outside of the local church where authenticity is less of a liability and creating a table big enough for pastors and ordinary people who don't have their spiritual shit together. Sandra's absence from her community isn't helping the people who are still there, it isn't making the greater Church any more God-honoring, and it certainly hasn't shown her the respect she deserves.

The ironic thing about stories like Sandra's is that from the Israelite patriarch Moses to the Old Testament prophet Elijah, to King David, to Jesus' disciple Thomas, to the man with the sick son, the Scriptures are filled with people who wear their doubt openly and who are regarded as caretakers of their religious tradition. Someone should tell those who invited Sandra to an early retirement. Someone should remind us when are ashamed of our struggles and we edit ourselves to feel we belong.

One of the things that happens as you seek to expand the table and experience the theological deconstruction that often comes with it is that you begin to see the Scriptures with new eyes. You come to them with a new openness, and you end up surprised by stories you thought you knew or discover words that had somehow been invisible before. One of my favorite passages from the fourteenth chapter of Mark's biography of Jesus tells the story of a woman breaking open a bottle of expensive perfume and anointing Jesus with it, while those around her protest passionately (14:3–9). The story begins with these simple words: "While he was at Bethany in the house of Simon the leper, as he sat at the table . . ."

I'd studied this passage, I'd led retreats around it, and I'd preached it numerous times—and yet for decades I'd missed this. Maybe it's because I got used to approaching the Bible the way so many Christians do, feeling as though I knew what it was about before reading it: *this* story illustrated *this* point. A fresh revelation from God wasn't nearly as important as me reinforcing what I already believed and wanted to teach, and so I often breezed through these eleven words of scene setting in my haste to get to the story of the woman and her reckless, audacious display of affection for Jesus, and I overlooked the fact that this introductory phrase *is* a story in itself. These few seemingly unimportant words are potentially world altering for us as we think about the table we would set in our lives and ministries. That Jesus is the houseguest and table companion of one of the most ostracized, most reviled, least respected members of the community was scandalous then and is revelatory for us now. In a time when lepers were required to announce themselves in the streets as "unclean" to avoid rubbing up against and contaminating the pure, morally superior folks, Jesus was pronouncing him worthy of fellowship, and in this way declaring *all* of us worthy. The Messiah and the leper at the table together: the gravity of this and the challenge it lays before us cannot be overstated.

Chances are you've known what it's like to be made the leper in the gathering of God's people. You've been pushed to the periphery because of some portion of your truth. You've been penalized for a season of your story. Or perhaps you've disconnected from those you deem unclean or unworthy or beyond redemption. Either side of this separation is equally damaging. Jesus' gathering at Simon's table becomes healing for us in our personal mess and our isolation as we seek welcome and as we grieve our rejection, and *equally confounding* in our own personal bigotry when we would withhold this welcome from someone else. And this is why total authenticity needs to be a nonnegotiable as we form or renovate our spiritual communities, because anything less distorts the image of Jesus and is disobedient to his example. There is nothing at all redemptive about a church made up of selectively authentic people, and nothing gained in acceptance built on redaction.

I'd been an honest guy before ministry because I could afford to be. There was no cost to transparency back then, no penalty to be assessed, no large-scale separation to fear. I could share myself fully and feel fairly secure that I was safe to do so. Somehow I'd lost the courage to be *that* person the deeper

I stepped into the Church. One of the gifts that being fired and rebooting my life and ministry gave me was the realization that I could, for the first time in decades, ask anything and say everything. No question was off the table and no conclusion was a deal breaker, and when you get a taste of this spiritual journey you'll never settle for less than that again. Can you imagine how liberating it must have been to Simon to have Jesus dine with him though he'd been the outcast in his own community, the validation of that kind of affirmation for someone so used to experiencing disdain? This is the freedom our spiritual communities should be marked by. This is the affirmation we should be giving. People should be able to ask anything and to say everything too, to be the most naked, real, vulnerable version of themselves and to know that they are safe as they do. This is the place the table needs to expand to.

U2 singer Bono recently commented on the lack of honesty in the Christian music industry: "I would love if this conversation would inspire people who are writing these beautiful . . . gospel songs, [to] write a song about their bad marriage. Write a song about how they're pissed off at the government. Because that's what God wants from you, the truth."[*] He's hit the nail squarely on the head in a way that is both refreshing and revelatory, saying what so many both inside and outside the Church have either realized for years but couldn't say or struggled to find words for. He just didn't go far enough. It isn't just the musicians in organized Christianity who are guilty of this voluntary editing. No, it's a far more pervasive virus than that. The Church itself has an authenticity problem. We have a very limited capacity to bear truth, and we so easily dismiss leaders and marginalize pew sitters when they reveal too much.

And it's a shame all around. The Church is capable of being a beautifully restorative community, one where disparate people are invited to bring the full weight of their inconsistency and hypocrisy and vacillation and to be lovingly received as

---

[*]Carol Kuruvilla, "Bono Wants Christian Music to Get More Honest," *Huffington Post*, April 27, 2016.

they are. It can and should be a place of loving renovation and healing and growth, but only when we allow everyone— both up front and in the pews—to be exactly who they are, to ask the truest questions of their hearts, to confront the deepest recesses of their personal darkness. It should be the very last place that pretending should be required or encouraged. And the wonderful truth is, a God worthy of worship can totally handle such naked honesty. It's sad when we who call ourselves the Church cannot.

At North Raleigh Community Church, where I've made my home and ministered for the past three years, we cuss a lot: in small groups, in casual conversation, even from the pulpit (well, it's actually a podium, but you get the idea). When I initially arrived, this was all a little disorienting to me, not because the words weren't part of my daily vernacular or because they offended my tender sensibilities, but because I knew better than to admit that I ever said such words or to utter them in mixed religious company. During our first Sunday visit, the pastor dropped an expletive during his message, and I nearly soiled myself. People laughed heartily, but no one seemed particularly surprised and no one walked out. I figured it was an accidental oversight—that is, until the next week. More expletives. I remember thinking, "This is brilliant. He's set the table for us all. He's letting us know that we all can be real here, that we are all in this together, and so we can let our guard down and be *exactly* who we are without pretense. We can be completely effing honest—and it's OK."

One of the ways we practically cultivate this unrestrained honesty in our community is with our Life Story groups. People gather over the course of a few weeks with relative strangers, with one person chosen each week to share whatever parts of their personal journey they decide to present. The rest of the group simply listens. They are not there to critique or push back or refute anything, but only to sit with and honor another person's story. The goal of the gatherings is to create space where everyone can be the most real version of themselves and know that they have a place at the table. When you're sure that your truest truth really is welcomed, you want to share yours. You *want* to be fully known. This is the heart of our church: the only person you need to be is the one you are at any given moment; flawed, failing, fearful, and loved by God and by those you gather with. Trust me when I tell you that it's heaven on earth.

Community, spiritual or otherwise, is only redemptive to the degree that we are fully seen and known when we partake in it, when we no longer feel burdened to pretend, when guilt or shame or fear are no longer a threat. When we can bring our truest selves without redaction, then we are really free. This is the table that Jesus invites us to. This is the table his example demands we set for the world. We, the filthy lepers, all get to dine with a Messiah, and none of us need to be clean.

9

True Diversity

C. S. Lewis said of forgiveness, "Everyone says forgiveness is a lovely idea, until they have something to forgive."* Similarly, every church on the planet claims to desire, seek, and welcome diversity—until real, messy, *diverse* diversity shows up at the door looking for a home, and then there's suddenly no room in the inn. Most faith communities and those leading them have a *diversity threshold*, a limited level of difference that they will tolerate comfortably. Beyond that point, they will be either subconsciously or overtly resistant to it. Very few churches are as open as advertised. Now, this shouldn't be surprising, because in many ways churches are no different from any assembly of flawed members of humanity who gather. They are essentially sprawling collections of a billion imperfections, biases, and wounds all trying to coexist in close quarters and, in this case, to hopefully do so in a way that reflects the character of God. In many ways faith communities are deeper than family because they are *chosen* kin, but this reality also brings a great potential for conflict because participants are working

* C. S. Lewis, *Mere Christianity*, rev. ed. (San Francisco: HarperSanFrancisco, 2001), 115.

with a lot less information about the other; they have very little equity of trust built up, and unlike blood family, it's a lot easier to take off when things go sideways.

In the Church we're trying to have the deepest community but beginning on a superficial level, which means eventually it isn't about magic, but about real, costly, difficult work. It's important for us to fully acknowledge this, since overspiritualizing our faith community is to imagine that simply because those assembled outwardly claim Christ, they all are fully capable of responding in his likeness, or to assume that faith automatically breeds effusive affection for those who are different. That's how we'd like it to work and often how we sell people on how it works, but in reality it's a bloody battle in the trenches to try and bear with people we see as unbearable, to love people we find decidedly unlovable. Part of this difficult work will involve moving beyond immediately categorizing people by their religious or political convictions. The tenor of our current *all-or-nothing* discourse tends to generate contempt for another simply because of the church they belong to or their voting bloc or their skin color or their sexual orientation. This is perhaps most true in the American Church, where you are what you believe or what your religion teaches you to believe about others. Real diversity needs to be a nonnegotiable of the bigger table, but it's never accomplished without intention, self-examination, and brutal honesty about ourselves at every given moment. These things are difficult to manage individually or in the context of a marriage, family, or friendship, let alone in an ever-changing group of irregular people seeking to be in community with one another.

The recent election revealed something about our church here in Raleigh that we shouldn't have been surprised by but were: we are *really* diverse, politically speaking. Nearly everyone came to our community after experiencing the worst parts of organized religion, beginning their exodus after finding they could no longer endure the rigid fundamentalism they experienced in church in the Bible Belt. Yet while they had jettisoned a conservative faith perspective on their way here, many still quietly held tightly to some historically conservative political values. This became apparent as people began to process the incredibly raw emotions at the conclusion of the campaign and as people began publicly owning their vote. The news came as a shock for many progressives in our community as they realized that they weren't in a completely "blue" church, as they had imagined; they had been living and worshiping alongside those whose vote now made them adversaries. The days and weeks following the election were marked by a new uneasiness for our community, in which we had to redouble our efforts to live with the open table we've always said we believe in, and we've had to navigate the brutally precarious road that marks an inclusive community. In the aftermath of November 8, we discovered that diversity is a wonderful but messy proposition, especially once it reaches beyond what you've imagined your limit to be.

This kind of inclusion and navigating of difference is costly and fraught with struggle—something they don't talk about very often in seminary. It requires tremendous sacrifice of time, of ease, of agenda, of preference. To an institutional church more and more used to measuring itself by corporate markers and with less and less area in the margins, diversity can seem to be counterproductive because it slows the machine down; it asks hard questions, it generates different conversations, it requires new systems. These things are all selfish time stealers, and they don't care about the fact that Sunday is always coming and stuff just needs to get done. They aren't worried about being a burden to the regularly scheduled program. They will not be content with whatever leftover bandwidth is available once all the "important church work" has been tended to. Because of this, the work of diversity is often left as only a noble aspiration that hopes the desire for inclusive community is itself enough to create it—and usually it isn't.

Earlier on our journey, the large church in suburban Charlotte where I spent nearly a decade named as one of our core values that we would be "full on, full color," meaning that we would embrace and pursue a diversity that we believe reflects heaven. Again, this in itself isn't a novel idea; in fact, it's part of any decent church's ministry basic starter kit. It's an idea that our pastors and staff and lay leadership all believed in, but we also knew that this conviction alone wouldn't be enough to make it so in our community; it would require more than just the desire for diversity. It would require explicit, repeated language from the pulpit. It would require continual messages from the platform. We would need to illustrate the diversity we wanted in our printed materials, on our ministry teams, in our staff hires, and we would need to be relentless in making sure that our community represented the diversity outside our doors as best as it could. Yet we also knew that all of these things would ultimately not be enough if our people didn't live diversity in the daily bread of real, deep, mutually enriching relationships.

As in many cases in the local church, the stuff that happens Monday through Saturday is the real sacred ground and the truest measure of ministry success. Even a diverse worship service can mask a more segregated day-to-day experience and make you believe you're doing the work of the Lord, when in reality you might just be putting on a great show that lots of people enjoy. Our leadership team knew that while standing in a crowd alongside a huge cross section of humanity and singing together for an hour certainly had value, that alone didn't mean that members of our community were invested in one another's lives and seeking to understand the oneness that connects us all. That was where we continually did our greatest work.

One of the truths we operated under was that people are naturally disarmed by serving together. When you place disparate folks alongside one another to do something meaningful, they aren't preoccupied or hindered by their differences, and in fact begin to see the great value in those differences. We leveraged much of our time and energy into doing good work together in the community, not only because it's a tangible way to replicate the life of Jesus, but also because it allows people space to learn truer stories about those they worship with and those they serve. There's an organic learning about *the other* that takes place that couldn't happen in even the most carefully crafted sermon. We didn't always get our efforts to foster diverse community right, but we got it right a whole lot, and as a result, year by year our corporate table expanded and our people began to embrace difference in their midst. And this is the fruit of such rich community: you realize how much less vivid your image of God had been before, how much deeper your understanding of the character of Christ becomes when you see it.

I still remember a Thursday afternoon still-life session back in art school. As we prepared to capture in paper and pigment the rather mundane assortment of pottery and fruit sprawled over some simple fabric, our professor told us that the key to being a great artist is appreciating the treasure hidden in the ordinary that other people miss and making them aware of it. And the greatest secret to this deeper seeing, he said, was to "become a student of what you were drawing"; to learn as much as you could from your subject, to find reverence for even the seemingly most unspectacular things. Not just for the ceramic pitcher dominating the still life, but for the way the drying leaf of the pear was beginning to curl or the way the light was reflecting up from the weathered patina of the table. The artist should be intimately aware of the specific beauty of whatever he or she is looking at and draw others' attention to it. Part of becoming people of a bigger table is having these same eyes for the people in our path, understanding that each person reveals another facet of divinity if we are willing to look deeply.

Our church staff's dream of being a "full color" community was completely dependent on our people seeking to be learners of one another's stories, believing that these stories would be blessings to be invited into. This is where diversity is cultivated. That's not to say that there weren't challenges and hiccups for us, and the bigger table ensures these moments. We each have blind spots, those places where we don't see our own resistance to variation, the voices we'd rather not hear, the newness we'd prefer not to embrace. But communities and families who believe that Jesus pulls us toward more expansive places will do that work that others won't. We were doing that work consistently, although the compromises of large church ministry still prevented us from reaching the most marginalized communities, those whose inclusion would prove messy for our relatively comfortable, suburban middle-class Bible Belt congregation. We had simultaneously a desire to create a bigger table and the inherent aversion to turbulence that high-functioning ministries come with. We wanted to welcome a disparate community, but we wanted it on our time line and without too much disturbance to the plan. Jesus' plan in the Gospels was marked by such disturbance to people's plans.

Real diversity often comes disguised as a problem. When disparate groups of people intersect, there is going to be turbulence, and the common danger, especially in faith communities, lies in believing that this turbulence is something unhealthy to be avoided. Faced with such tasks as deciding how church funds should be allocated, navigating a response to controversial local legislation, debating theological positions, or determining what kind of music to have on Sunday mornings, many Christians read any discomfort as reason to abort discussion because these conversations must be pleasant and easy to be faith affirming. In reality, this discomfort is the fierce crucible of redemptive spiritual community and what we should be seeking, because it means that we are straining to include those still excluded and that we are seeking to make our abstract faith work in a real and messy daily existence. As we experience and learn to incorporate our differences, we find patience, we see the complexity of God's beauty, and most importantly we find our greatest commonality in Christ. This is the very lifeblood of the Body, and it is worth whatever we have to postpone or discard to tend to it. The early Church never wanted for interpersonal conflict, but it also never shied away from it, because this friction was and still is the necessary by-product of continually inviting outsiders in and making room for the way they think, worship, live, and see the world, and allowing these things to alter the community. The Church is not a static thing that we ask people to discard their individuality to join; it is a living organism that we invite them to connect with and change with their presence. It is always *becoming*.

One of the greatest pieces of ministry advice I've ever received came from Kara Powell, executive director of the Fuller Youth Institute, who said, "If you want students to feel significant, give them something significant to be a part of." This is one of the deepest truths there is when it comes to churches and ministries with regard to their mission, and it's also been one of the purest paths to real diversity. One of the greatest barriers to welcoming difference is simply boredom. When local churches don't have compelling enough work to be part of, their people get lazy and default to a consumer mind-set, to easy community, to surface affinities. They will fall back on labels, and they will gradually shrink the table.

I oversaw a massive youth ministry in Charlotte, with hundreds of students and dozens of volunteers participating each week. We had tons of programming, really great engagement from parents, wonderful church support, and by most measurements were really successful. But as our youth staff looked at our students and our ministry more closely, beneath all the activity and energy we realized that we were still all about us; our diversity was only what the bigger church was feeding us. We began imagining what it would look like to really move out of the building and off the campus, and to connect to the movement of justice already happening in our city. We wondered how we could tangibly expand the table. By the end of the afternoon we'd created Spring Breakthrough, an alternative spring break in which teams of students would partner with local ministries in the community, not asking people to come to us, but joining them at the tables they were already setting. We were really excited by the prospect, but unsure if it would fly with our fairly well-to-do suburban students, who, like most folks, leaned a bit more toward self than other. We put together a pitch, and later that week we made the invitation. By the time we began day one of Spring Breakthrough a few weeks later, we had 125 students who served at forty sites throughout Charlotte, feeding people, fixing stuff, spending time with people, hosting block parties.

The week began with a prayer walk through the inner city, with students carrying care bags filled with snacks, water, toiletry items, and socks. The bags themselves were a way to meet a physical need and also to open the door for conversation with strangers—not evangelism per se, but an opportunity to let people know they were seen and loved, and that they mattered. Our teens were to give several of these care bags out, but not without learning names, asking people to share their story, and asking if they needed prayer or a hug. I can still remember standing in Uptown Charlotte, looking in every direction and seeing dozens of teenagers talking, praying, and eating with strangers. It was about as humbling a moment as I've ever experienced. It began what would be a beautiful week, but this was far more than a ministry event for us. This was a complete heart transplant in real time. It was catalytic for our student ministry because it turned us all outward, and it showed our leadership team that when people are fully invested together in redemptive work, their differences are only a beautiful addition to that work, never a detriment to it. Too many churches have a diversity problem, but this is because they have a vision problem.

Real diversity demands that we hold loosely our preconceived ideas of what God looks like. Jesus didn't dine with the sinners so that he could convert them all to Pharisees, but to remind the Pharisees that God speaks as loudly through prostitutes as he does through them. He was validating every story, always elevating the other. He was destroying the myth that spirituality needs to be dressed in the trappings of religion, that it has to be proper or conventional or uniform. We still struggle with this work because we are naturally a people of labels, always looking for neat and tidy ways of summarizing those who cross our paths, of easily categorizing them for quick understanding. Our labels help reinforce the ideas of who's in and who's out and make us feel safely sequestered in what we believe comprises our tribe. The problem is that people are far too expansive for any category we might place them in, and because of this all our efforts of relational shorthand fail. Whether our labels reference race, gender, sexual orientation, theology, or any other designation, they place in front of us a caricature of what we imagine that label represents—and they always fall short.

For much of my life I've been a die-hard Prince fan. I didn't start that way, though. On March 30, 1985, I was standing a few blocks from the Carrier Dome in Syracuse, New York. My friend Ed and I had gone to pick up his girlfriend after Prince's sold-out show there. It was the Purple Rain Tour, the concert had been simulcast around the country, Princesanity was in full effect here and all over the world—and I couldn't have cared less. "Look at these freaks," I thought to myself as I watched the purple throng filling the sidewalks. I was pretty much a rocker at the time, preferring the slightly less nuanced, riff-laden musical stylings of Judas Priest and Iron Maiden. Sure, I dug the blazing guitar solo in "Let's Go Crazy" (who didn't?), but for the most part I didn't connect with Prince: the androgyny, the salaciousness, the stratospheric falsetto— I just didn't get it. Fast-forward a couple of years, and it all clicked. I'd moved to Philadelphia, and as my world expanded with diversity I'd never experienced before, Prince became the most fitting soundtrack. His songs were my companion as I discovered how big life could be and just what diversity could look like. I had the good fortune of seeing Prince a dozen times or so, and the experience was euphoric and spiritual in ways that are difficult to quantify. I remember the first time I stood in Philadelphia's Tower Theater, crammed tightly in the middle of a dancing, pulsating mass, thinking, "These are my people!" It turns out I felt at perfectly at home with the freaks. This was family. And among so many other gifts, this was the real magic of Prince. He brought completely disparate groups of humanity together and made them feel they fit. He transcended musical genres and broke through color lines and challenged gender roles, and he boldly declared the dance floor big enough for all of us and open all night. And in that free and joyful place, we all danced. When you were at a Prince show, you belonged. You were the right color, the right shape, the right religion, the right you. And in that space you felt at home in your own skin and deeply connected to those around you in ways that defy explanation.

This should be what the Church gives people. It should give them a place. It should be the spot where all prodigals feel they've come home. It should be the building with the biggest table. We've been led to believe that the goal of equality is to somehow make differences disappear, yet in reality it is to be profoundly aware of them and to recognize them as beautiful and valuable and necessary. The virtue is not in ignoring our various distinctions but in celebrating them; not in pretending as though they don't exist, but in believing that their existence makes us a better version of humanity as we live together in community. Yes, there is much about us that is universal: the desire to be heard and known, the need to be loved and to love, the joy of finding our place and purpose, and the need to live into these without restraint. Championing equality is to see every person as fully deserving of such things and to work so that each can pursue them with as little obstacle as possible from both without and within. Yet we also need to realize and name the ways in which equality is not a default setting in the world and to acknowledge the very real barriers many experience simply because of the color of their skin or their gender identity or their land of origin.

This is the reason that saying "all lives matter" is an irresponsible and poor response to #BlackLivesMatter, the movement to fight the injustices faced by people of color. To specifically affirm black lives is to speak directly into a system that operates and has operated as if those lives matter far less. It's purposefully and explicitly lifting up the inherent humanity of those who have been and still are being treated inhumanely. Saying that black lives matter acknowledges the blind spots white people have inherited that prevent us from noticing our privilege, advantages, and biases—and the way all these things conspire to make us much more tolerant of

African Americans' deaths, much more likely to rationalize them away, and much more likely to get over them quickly. When we say #BlackLivesMatter, we don't need to also simultaneously say #WhiteLivesMatter to somehow model moral consistency or keep the table bigger. Our nation has been morally inconsistent, and that is the *very* point. That white lives matter in America has never been in question a single day of our existence, so we really don't need to say it. White people have never *not* mattered in the process. We can build a bigger table while simultaneously critiquing those already at the table or realities that prevent everyone from gathering.

While attending a conference for LGBTQ Christians, I was in the coffee shop in the hotel lobby talking with a young lesbian woman about equality, compassion, faith—about the bigger table. Just outside the window where we were sitting stood a man carrying a large sign that assured this girl that she was going to hell. I'll call him Sign Guy. He was yelling and pacing and quite clearly there to preach and not to listen. The girl looked at me and asked, "So how do I respond to that? How do I love Sign Guy?" (I was sort of hoping I could phone a friend.) I thought about it a second and suggested that for her and me, the key is to try and see one fundamental similarity between us and the man: that we are all trying to do the very same thing at this very moment, to hear and respond to the voice of God that we hear in our heads. So while Sign Guy's methods and manner are outwardly quite horrible, and while they are coming across as violent, hateful, and intolerant, *in his mind at this moment* he is doing exactly what we are doing right now. He is trying to be faithful to whatever image of God he's inherited. No one ever thinks, "I am doing this wrong." Everyone believes that they are living and responding out of genuine faith. So we try and understand the fear and the lack of understanding that created Sign Guy. He wasn't born a Sign Guy. I asked my friend if we could see that shared desire to know God as enough common ground to expand the table, even to someone like that. Can that very small space be enough to begin a conversation? But here's the problem: if I ask a fifty-five-year-old Southern

Baptist sign guy and a sixteen-year-old lesbian girl to sit down at the table, it is a far greater risk for the girl because it is costing her much more, because her very identity is under attack from the other. So while we call people together to the table, we don't ignore the injustices already at play in their lives.

Our distinctions of race, gender, orientation, and place of origin all shape how easy or difficult it has been for us to claim the same inherent needs we have to be seen and heard and respected, and they craft the specific lens through which we filter the world. The very specific intersection of our various differences alters how we individually have experienced life, and so we need to bring these all to bear as we build community, each being informed by one another. The color of someone's skin, their inclination to love, their gender identity, the culture of their upbringing, and every other facet of their humanity matter, because these all work in concert to compose the once-in-history expression of life they manifest. These things are the unique lines of their original stories.

And as a person of faith, these distinctions all reveal the unlimited beauty of One who is the source of each of us, so this rich diversity is the very holy ground where God speaks. Bigotry doesn't happen when we notice other people's differences. It happens when we believe or act as if those differences make another less worthy of love or opportunity or compassion or respect. We need to learn to dance together.

10

Agenda-Free Community

Regardless of your financial situation, life stage, personality type, or any other variable, shopping for a car is a fairly universally loathed experience, just below open-heart surgery without an anesthetic. (My apologies to my beloved salesperson friends out there, but that's just the truth.) What people hate the most about the whole ordeal is the idea that they're getting *sold* from the second they walk in the door. The lobby, the signage, the background music, the layout of the building, and the warm, folksy banter are all designed for one purpose: *closing the deal.* The salespeople, as honest or sincere as they may be, all have a clearly defined objective, a reason for being there: *selling to you.* They want to meet you, disarm you, persuade you to feel your pressing need for what they have, and get you under contract before you walk out the door—and they'll say and do just about anything to make that happen.

It's an art form, really. These people have done their homework and they know their business, and that business is to build relationship, to engender trust, and to get the dotted line signed before you leave. Good salespeople know how to manipulate your emotions and how to overcome the obstacles you may place in their path, and they understand the power that words have in convincing people to say yes, even when their minds are still at best a soft maybe. Their one purpose is securing that affirmative decision, and so whatever connection it feels like they're building with you, it's all a means to *that* end. That's why, once you buy a car or you walk out the door without doing so, you rarely hear from them again. They've already done what they've been asked to do.

Most people don't walk into churches thinking they're being sold to, but often they are. They don't realize that the space they step into on a given Sunday has been as carefully crafted as any local car dealership, with experienced professionals there for a purpose. As they welcome visitors, there is a goal, there is a *product*, and there is a clear objective: closing that deal, which is usually framed as some variation on a "decision for Christ," church membership, financial commitment, or ministry participation. From the worship gatherings to the Web site content to the words spoken from the pulpit or platform, everything is done for one reason: to facilitate an easy, predictable, hopefully immediate yes to Jesus, and some measurable involvement in the church community that verifies it. You may be thinking, "Well, they're churches, isn't that the point? Isn't that what they're supposed to do? Isn't that the very heart of the Great Commission?" (Matt. 28:16–20). Well, maybe it is and maybe it isn't. This may not be quite the Church as it was envisioned by Jesus, or the one that sprung up in his wake. That one was far more enigmatic and far less calculated, involving the mysterious stuff of parables about the kingdom of God and about a people living with awareness of its presence in and around them.

Before it was ever an institution, before it was a massive entertainment compound, before it was a weekend mountaintop destination, the Church was a community, one whose lifeblood was real, authentic, interdependent relationships. People gathered together to bear one another's burdens, to worship and learn and serve, and to work out together how the words and ministry of Jesus translated into the ordinary lives of those who sought to follow after him. It was an organic evolution; that beautifully insidious "yeast in the dough" Jesus talked about (Matt. 13:33). There was no program, no guide, no Three Steps to Salvation. The wild, unpredictable movement of the Spirit of God hadn't yet been dissected, branded, and packaged for mass consumption and global franchising. An odd collection of humanity came together daily to share stories, to break bread, and to encourage one another. The "Church" was simply the natural by-product of followers of Christ living together. It was the uniquely sweet yield of disparate people knowing one another and being known. These relationships became the very heart of the spiritual communities they birthed and the recognizable and captivating thing about them to the watching world. This was the source of the Church's exponential growth. Their greatest testimony was their intertwined lives, not their buildings or their brand or their vacation Bible school.

The book of Acts (part of the Gospel of Luke, though now separated from it by the Gospel of John in the Bible) gives us vivid imagery of the way daily existence and faith were connected and shows us a Church with a goal that was far more holistic and far less myopic than merely an altar call or a Sinner's Prayer or even some measurable behavior modification. People were living together in a way that perpetuated the way of Jesus, and this beautiful presence was going viral because their open table reminded people of his. A disparate group found equal welcome in his unconditionally loving presence, and community was created. At first glance, that would seem to be what the average Sunday worship gathering seeks to reproduce. However, if you dig a little deeper beneath the coffee bars and bookstores and rock-band aesthetic of the megachurch or the sweet, folksy charm of smaller churches, you'll find that far too often, everything is setting the stage for the "big ask," that critical conversion moment that has become the cap feather for churches and pastors. The hub of our modern faith communities is no longer the rather tedious, sometimes boring, slow building process of nurturing deep relationships, but rather an hour of faith-based programming designed to pull the heartstrings and generate some simple, measurable data that disciples are being made.

Of the many stories I hear from former Christians and wandering faith refugees from the traditional Church, this is among the most common: the realization that their earlier inclusion was highly conditional and their relationships little more than surface decoration. When push came to shove and life got messy, they were discarded or forgotten. So many people are warmly welcomed in the front door of the church and later, without fanfare or protest, simply slide out the back door—or are tossed out. When we approach people like raw material for salvation machines, it shouldn't be surprising that they feel like a number.

It isn't just churches and pastors that have this attitude. This sales mind-set invariably spills over into the seats and small groups and into the interactions of the people in these communities. "Leading people to Christ" has become one of the fundamental ways Christians now measure their personal faithfulness too, and it is this ulterior motive that so often runs in the background operating systems of our relationships and becomes the subtext for how we relate to people, especially those outside the church campus. In fact, this is the very heart of evangelism as we've learned it, preached it, and taught it to our faith communities. As a result, people outside the church building often feel like (because in reality they are) religious "projects" taken on by Christians: doomed, lost souls needing to be rescued. They are looked at not as image bearers of God with stories to tell and wisdom to share, but as damned souls to be saved from hell. Again, connecting people to Christ sounds like and is a rather noble endeavor, but the truth is that this has devolved into an oversimplified transaction. It's led to faith communities where people don't matter as much as the souls they represent.

One blistering June afternoon I sat across from Steven, my then pastor, in a Raleigh café. I was sharing my frustration with the great amount of ministry for students we were doing in the building and the noticeable lack of it in the city itself, with how little we were out beyond the campus caring for the community and how inwardly focused our students were. His answer was that if we wanted to be out in the community, then we should do more "evangelistic events," which meant basically taking our slick Sunday salvation show out on the road. Steven told me that the "social justice thing" was all well and good but that it wasn't saving anyone. (I really wanted to break out the Gospels and just start reading out loud as a rebuttal but I had enough self-awareness to realize that probably wouldn't go well.) Instead I pivoted in our conversation and started telling stories about the pastoral care our ministry staff was doing for our teens, describing the sea of dysfunctional marriages, addiction, self-harm, and depression that we were currently drowning in. I saw it as symptomatic of our community at large: lots of hurting people who were seriously in need of care, far more than entertainment. He said to me quite matter-of-factly, "John, it isn't an exaggeration to say that I have absolutely zero interest in ministering to people." I think I had an aneurysm, but I kept a poker face and quickly sipped my artisan ginger ale.

In a few seconds this pastor had summed up what agenda-based community in the Church yields: a burning desire to "get people saved" and general apathy to them beyond that. We become fixated on people's eternal souls but don't give much of a damn about the rest of their earthly lives. We convince ourselves that salvation is grasped only in an altar call and not in the million ordinary moments where we live and breathe with an awareness of the presence of God.

We have so distilled the sprawling experience of lifelong faith down to one tiny, measurable moment that we've forgotten how much living alongside people Jesus actually did. We wrongly imagine the Gospel stories as one continual, thirty-three-year tent revival, a never-ending rock-show crusade, and we miss the reality that the pages of the story of Jesus are filled with quiet conversations, with walks in the field, with hands upon weary shoulders, with loving meals around the table.

We forget the wounds that were mended, the feet that were washed, the bread that was broken. These were as real and powerful and life altering as any tearful worship service prayer. Yes, Jesus preached on the hillsides and in the towns and in the synagogues, but if that were all he did, we'd have a far shorter New Testament. He seemed to have as much reverence for the table as he did the tabernacle.

We had hundreds of students in our community, and since they were raised in the Southeast most of them had said the Sinner's Prayer before (many of them a few dozen times, probably), but they were still a steaming mess: still struggling for identity, still desperate for belonging, still battling their demons. They certainly weren't *finished*. But from the outside they were considered "saved," and with their eternal destination secured, the rest seemed far less important to Pastor Steven. Regardless of their struggles and their youth and their immature faith, they were expected to get on with the work of "bringing people to Christ," of replicating the experience they'd had. In other words, despite their damage, despite their dysfunction, and despite what they might or might not know about the faith they claimed publicly at some point, they were being drafted into repeating the same kind of event-based, agenda-heavy spirituality they'd walked into. I left that café feeling as though I was an alien in my own church, and I knew my time there was short. I'd finally exhausted my capacity to tolerate phony relationship as a way of selling people salvation.

But maybe there is a better path to building community and to being in redemptive relationships with people, one where we come not to change or fix or convert them, but simply to reflect Christ to them and trust *that* is enough. What if leading people to Jesus wasn't about closing the deal with a magic prayer or getting them to come tearfully down a church aisle in the manufactured urgency of lights and crescendoing worship songs? What if sharing the gospel is really a matter of giving people a daily front-row seat to a life that looks like Christ? What if the way we *best* make disciples is by showing people the fullest incarnation of Jesus that we can manage and resting in that? We who are working on building a bigger table are beginning to believe that the best evangelism is letting people know that we follow Jesus—and then not being a complete jerk. It's a pretty low bar, really. This is the cry of so many who now find themselves outside of organized religion yet who are still yearning for spiritual nurturing. If we spend our lives in honest, loving, mutually beneficial relationships with people, is that enough? If our compassion, forgiveness, and encouragement don't yield some quantifiable "decision for Jesus," is it a waste, or is there redemptive work simply in living life alongside people and seeking? I believe millions of people are saying yes.

Every day I speak with people from every faith tradition, with nonreligious people, and with Christians all along the theological spectrum who are starved for real, authentic community. They are finding it in a myriad of places—online and in homes and through social gatherings—or they are creating it themselves by taking the very best things they've experienced in religious traditions, while avoiding the parochialism or coercion that they've encountered. They are building diverse gatherings that allow for difference and paradox. They've decided to hold tightly to love, support, belonging, and mutual respect—while letting go of the propensity to homogenize people or convert them.

This chapter may all sound like a cynical attack on the Church from just another disgruntled, burned-out pastor, but I hope you realize that it isn't. I still spend every Sunday in the local church. I've experienced the best of what it can be. I know that all faith communities (including those in which I've served) are filled with good, passionate, faithful people trying to love other people well. For the vast majority of ministers, church leaders, and members, the ulterior motives at work are pure and wonderful, but they are present just the same. They alter the way relationships are framed and cultivated. I say these things without malice or bitterness, because I think we can do better. We who are working to expand the table are seeing how transformative this is all the way around, the blessing that flows in all directions. When we who claim faith come to people without any agenda other than to receive them as they are and to love them as they desire to be loved, they rest in the safety of that, and they begin to be transformed without prodding or direction from us.

As we who already comprise the Church recalibrate our hearts for a different purpose, we are beautifully altered too. When we treasure people as they are, we become less manipulative; we become better listeners; we are less prone to morality policing. Agenda-free community allows messiness and failure and regression in ways that are so rarely tolerated in the traditional church. Again, this is the table Christ sets over and over in the Scriptures: the place of continual restoration, perennial communion, unending fellowship. You don't earn a spot there; you don't fail and then find yourselves outside of it. Just ask Peter. He was one of Jesus' original twelve disciples, the one who publicly boasted of his faithfulness to his teacher, even if it meant his own death. It would be this same Peter who would soon stand in the public square following Jesus' arrest, denying three times that he even knew him. And the Gospel writer John describes this same Peter weeks later, standing on the shoreline, being forgiven three times by a resurrected Jesus, as a symbolic wiping away of his failure following a restorative waterside meal hosted by his teacher (John 21:15–22). This is the table Jesus sets. It is the table of second chances, and two hundredth chances, the table of grace. There you don't ever lose your place, and you are never "finished."

At the table, Jesus had wisdom to share, hard words to give, and purpose to call people to, but more than that he had their humanity to affirm. He allowed them the dignity of being seen and heard and known. Imagine what it would look like if we oriented ourselves around that pursuit, if we had no other agenda than walking alongside people sharing the view of God from where we stand, not needing them to see what we see, or believe what we believe, but to encounter Jesus in our very flesh.

PART THREE

Under Construction

11

Show Them the Ocean

For me, going to the beach is always like meeting God. There's that moment when you make your way down the path that cuts through the dunes. As you walk farther, the quiet noise in the distance gradually becomes a welcome roar. You crane your neck as if unsure it's all still there. Your pace quickens as the sound rises and the wind grows, and suddenly you're emptied out into the full, vivid majesty of it all. And you breathe. It never fails to level me. It is never commonplace. It is always holy ground. If you've been to the beach, you understand exactly what I mean. If you haven't—well, you just won't. That's the thing about the ocean: until you experience it, no one can explain it to you, and once you have experienced it, no one needs to. The love of God is this way. For far too long, Christians have been content with telling people about the ocean and believing that is enough.

We've spoken endlessly of a God whose lavish, scandalous love is beyond measure, whose forgiveness reaches from the furthest places and into our deepest personal darkness. We've spun gorgeous, fanciful tales of a redeeming grace that is greater than the worst thing we've done and available to anyone who desires it. We've talked about a Church that welcomes the entire hurting world openly with the very arms of Jesus. We've talked and talked and talked—and much of the time we've been a clanging gong, our lives and shared testimony making a largely loveless noise in their ears. They receive our condemnation. They know our protests. They experience our exclusion. They endure our judgment. They encounter our bigotry. And all of our flowery words ring hollow. It's little wonder they eventually choose to walk away from the shore, the idea as delivered through our daily encounters with them not compelling enough to pursue for themselves. Our commitments to hospitality, authenticity, diversity, and community can be empty words, too, if we don't put them into practice.

Church, the world doesn't need more talking from us. It doesn't need our sweet platitudes or our eloquent speeches or our passionate preaching or our brilliant exegesis. These are all just words about the ocean, and ultimately they fail to adequately describe it. The world needs the goodness of God incarnated in the flesh of the people who claim to know this good God. As they meet us, they need to come face-to-face with radical welcome, with unconditional love, with counterintuitive forgiveness. They need to experience all of this in our individual lives and in the Church, or they will decide that it is all no more than a beautiful but ultimately greatly exaggerated story about sand and waves and colors that cannot be described.

If we're not careful, religion can easily drift into abstraction, all becoming theoretical, speculative discussions about stuff that sounds good and spiritual but doesn't actually result in any substantive change, never moving from our hearts to our hands. In fact, most of us who have experienced some disconnection with organized religion would probably name this as one of our core frustrations: we see Christians making little difference in the world, or making a difference that feels more like harm. It was the impetus of my first exodus from the Church in my early twenties: everything that resonated with me about Jesus felt confined to a church service. I grew tired of having a

Sunday faith that had little value on Tuesday night or Friday afternoon. Participating in the local church began to feel like reading a glossy travel brochure about a place I really wanted to visit but couldn't ever have access to. I adored the aspirational aspects of my Christian community but rarely tasted the fruit. I loved hearing the stories of Jesus, reading about his compassion, seeing the way he seemed to be forever expanding the table, pulling up chairs so that the hurting and unseen and disregarded could be invited in. I was inspired by the way he dined with people and showed them their worth even when others denied it. But this Jesus seemed to stay confined to that book and to those stories, rarely leaving the church campus.

This has been one of the constant threads running through my entire spiritual journey: looking for ways to make the things of heaven work here on earth, to tangibly bring heaven down. Maybe you're still holding tightly to that same thread. Maybe you're finding affinity in these longings, in these dreams, in this hope for something more redemptive for our spiritual communities. I'm hoping that something in my story has caused your heart to amen loudly. And yet, like me, you've nearly used up your reserves of hope that such things are possible, that we can somehow bring something fundamentally new to a faith tradition already thousands of years old. This isn't about finding something that's trendy or sexy or novel—but something real that will stick.

I would imagine you're probably not wondering whether radical hospitality, total authenticity, true diversity, and agenda-free community are good or beautiful or needed. I'll wager we'd all agree that they are, in the same way we all agree that reflecting the character of Christ in the world is a really good idea. The question in matters of radically and tangibly living our faith is usually, "Where do we start?" And if we don't find a clear and compelling answer to that question rather quickly, we soon become frustrated, and we eventually place that urgency on the shelf along with the latest book we're reading until both gradually gather dust. Sooner or later we need to get out of the laboratory of our theology and get our hands dirty and see if the stuff we're talking about can work. Is this bigger table really possible?

For the past two years, people online and on the ground here in Raleigh have been trying to figure out just that. We are finding the progress to be painfully slow and have experienced plenty of fits and starts along the way—but the bigger table can only be built like this. This is not easy work, and probably the biggest reason for that is because of what we're *not* building. We're not replacing the institutional church with another version of it. We're not planting churches, we're not colonizing an area for Christ, we're not building franchises in the name of Jesus. These things have been done for decades—even centuries. They've been analyzed and studied and written about, and there are endless how-to resources to create a variation on this theme. What we're talking about is something far more difficult, far more time consuming, and far less measurable. We are both figuratively and literally inviting people to the table and holding the expectations loosely. We're starting with a few nonnegotiables (hospitality, authenticity, diversity, relationship) and trusting in the spirit of God to engineer and steer and define what that looks like through those who gather. Since the bigger table isn't about installing a ministry system, it's going to be more nebulous and more elusive than we have grown up believing church should be. In essence we are building a church backward. The institutionalized Church that so many people are walking away from or saying no to isn't necessarily evil or willfully sinful—it's just all turned around.

The template and sequence for birthing Christian faith communities has been shockingly predictable for a few decades:

1. Start with a Main Person (usually a guy—let's be honest) who will drive the whole thing. That person's charisma and speaking ability are paramount, because he will be the focal point, the declared or voted-upon visionary, and the face of the church. He will get the butts in the seats (or pews) on Sundays.

2. Put a Ministry Team around the Main Guy as support staff. This will be a group of talented, passionate people who will serve the needs of the Main Guy and the Main Guy's vision.

3. Find a building, choose service times, and get a band and tech team together. This building and these worship gatherings featuring this band and this crew will be the unquestionable hub of the new community, around which everything else revolves and toward which the lion's share of the community's personnel, budget, and energy will be marshaled. It is unequivocally the Main Event featuring the Main Guy.

4. Attach ancillary, age-based ministries (child care, children's ministry, student ministry, adult classes) around these worship gatherings. These are spokes from the central worship service hub, and they usually come only as necessary by-products of it.

5. Create small groups, aka community groups, designed to build relationships and help people develop intimate, meaningful community, since such intimacy will be increasingly challenging as the church grows numerically, which it is designed to do.

6. Create service ministries or mission programs to help people learn the value and virtues of caring for others.

In building most of our modern churches this way, we've made the wrong things—a personality and a production—the main things from the jump. We have created a top-heavy, corporate version of Christian community. This isn't what we're looking to replicate any longer.

We're looking to build organic faith communities that truly begin with relationships, to craft ways and spaces for people to come together to break bread and share stories naturally, and to let *that* be the hub of what a church does and becomes over time: The actual people dictate the system, the structure, the spending. The staff then take on the role of serving and encouraging the community to live out what is rising up in their midst. They become caretakers of the people's needs, spending more time in the trenches around kitchen tables, in the streets, and at bedsides than on the stage or in the pulpit or on social media. That's less sexy a role, but perhaps a healthier one for everyone involved, because it nurtures humility rather than inflates ego. In this way, a local church begins reflecting the hearts and desires of those gathered. It then allows everything it does to be informed by the community: what ministries it creates, what physical structures it invests in, how it spends its resources, and whether or not a corporate worship service is desirable—and if so, what that looks like. It is a far more participatory and collaborative endeavor. We don't function as leaders managing and controlling the thing from above, but as table setters who will experience the community as it takes shape. This is unfamiliar ground for many of us raised in a quantifiable, results-based Christianity that uses budgets, buildings, and baptism to measure its success.

I flew to California to lead a one-night table gathering to introduce this idea to a group of folks there and to give them a real-time experience of sitting across from people and working through some of what we're talking about here. The forty or so people gathered fully spanned the Christian theological spectrum, as well as some identifying as agnostic or atheist. I spent thirty minutes or so sharing my story (much of what you've read about in these pages) and laid out the idea of the bigger table and the four nonnegotiable "legs" of the table (hospitality, authenticity, diversity, relationship). Things began smoothly enough. Everyone listened and laughed and nodded with approval, and when I opened the floor to let people process, many who spoke first were the more progressive Christians who clearly had found lots of affinity in what I'd shared about frustrations with the institutional church and the desire for a more diverse Christian experience. Had this been a gathering of only such like-minded, theologically aligned people, there probably would have been some great dialogue, but it would have been—as faith communities so often are—a lot of preaching to the choir, an echo chamber of agreement. But the bigger table truly does desire disparate faith perspectives, and the room that night represented this—which is why the next hour got decidedly "prickly."

A more conservative Christian woman brought up the "inerrancy of Scripture," and tempered her support for diversity with the conviction that we can't let this make us reticent to "call people out on their sin." Before she could finish her sentence, an explosion of dissent shot out from a handful of LGBTQ-affirming folks present. A Christian in the process of deconstructing his faith began raising his voice to a near yell, pushing back on the woman's comments as typifying the prejudices that drove him from the Church. As the comments pingponged around the room and the emotional temperature shot up, another voice burst beyond it all. An atheist shared through tears how hesitant she'd been to show up that night and how sad the exchange made her, being so typical of the Christian rhetoric that had helped nudge her out of belief. There were quiet sobs, some stunned silence, and an awkwardness that fell over the room when everyone realized just how quickly things had escalated. Over the rest of our time together, we talked about the reality of what we'd just sat through and why it was perfect. It was an honest, passionate exchange where no one lost their dignity. It was messy, but it wasn't ugly. This is what the bigger table is. This is what we're talking about. It isn't a place to hear and parrot back a bunch of platitudes you agree with. It isn't about going to a building and consuming some pleasing faith-based entertainment. This is about sharing space with people who don't share your beliefs but who are willing to listen. The bigger table isn't one you run from at the first sign of discord. It is based on the lost sacred art of *staying*.

After the close of the evening, many people lingered to have follow-up conversations with me, to introduce themselves to one another, and to talk more about what the night had been like for them. I spent the next morning processing the previous evening over breakfast with the gathering's host, as well as attending to some of the collateral damage we'd incurred. The more conservative woman who'd initiated the heated exchange had left early and gone home feeling as though her respect for the Scriptures had been dismissed. When the conversation turned to sexual orientation, a gay man had felt marginalized by hearing people talk around him or about him—and not to him. I also had the chance to have coffee with a Christian who was stretching to be more affirming but who was hung up on some theological stuff that he wanted to talk through. It was a full and heavy day, but it wasn't at all discouraging. It's part of the process of expanding the table. Emotions will be volatile, wounds will be exposed, ideas will be challenged. If I'd had the luxury of living alongside these folks for more than a couple of days, this would be what community would look like. We gather and attend to needs, and gather again and repeat the process. There is no start and stop time, no final resolution, and no tidy little bow we can put on everything in an hour.

At our debrief on the last day of my trip, I reminded one of my new friends what we had experienced two nights earlier. An extremely diverse group of people gathered, more diverse than at any traditional church service. They heard other stories, and even though they didn't all agree with one another, they engaged in a way that was much more real and much more redemptive than they would online. They also now had faces and names to replace their doctrines and issues. Many of them exchanged numbers and were scheduling times to connect again in person or on social media. This is the fruit of just a day or two together. Can you imagine what a few months or years or a life of this could yield?

Expanding the table isn't for the faint of heart or the impatient, which is why so few people actually attempt it, but there is something transformative on the other side of it. When people are shown the ocean, they are changed in ways that words about the ocean could never come close to. This should be the heart of those of us who claim faith or who simply believe in living a practical theology of love. We need to stop talking and we need to walk shoulder to shoulder with people in real, messy, authentic community—until we all can see it for ourselves.

12

Bullies, Bibles, and Bullhorns

Your theology is overrated.

That's not to say that it's not important; it's just not as important as you probably think it is or have grown up believing. It's certainly not what the bigger table is about, but more importantly it's really not what this Christian life is about—at least if we're to use the Gospels as a reference point. Most of us have been conditioned to believe that our spirituality is all about our belief system—all the boxes we check, the way we interpret individual passages of the Bible, the clever and complicated ways we talk about God: our Christian apologetic. We normally lead with theology even if we're unaware of it. Invariably our litmus test for the depth and authenticity of a person's faith is likely what they *believe*, not who they are. We see their hermeneutic as more important than their character.

This is especially true in the forced distance of social media, where we quickly screen people for their take on the polarizing issues of the day—sexuality, abortion, guns, politics—and their responses determine how we evaluate their religious convictions and whether or not we want to be in spiritual community with them. We've lived so long in an Internet culture of drive-by analysis that we've forgotten that this isn't normal, that our faith demands a deeper investment of time, of ourselves. We never even make it to the table with many people because we've evaluated and judged them from a mile away. As a result, local churches so often become segregated, conditional communities of like-minded culture-warring Christians who believe they have God on their side. These faith communities rarely operate as one big table, just a series of smaller ones. Despite all our talk of a gospel for everyone, despite our effusive language about diversity and inclusion and grace for all—we ultimately just want to know what people think about gays or guns or maybe hell, and we either align ourselves with or distance ourselves from them depending on their answer. In this way theology becomes an easy, efficient barrier between ourselves and those we believe to be less enlightened than we are. Our belief system becomes a wall. Yet Jesus didn't have a theology, at least not in the way most Christians imagine he did or the kind they perceive for themselves.

In the fifth chapter of Matthew's biography, Jesus sits down on a rugged hillside packed with a mix of the devoted, the curious, and the skeptical and begins to teach. There are no programs, Bible apps, PowerPoint slides, or video bumpers. Many of those gathered likely had never heard him before, and they certainly hadn't read anything he'd written or been able to dissect his teachings. This is perhaps one of the most overlooked aspects of the life and ministry of Christ: the distinct lack of a "Christian" religion. There was no New Testament, after all, just the words being spoken in real time out of the very mouth of Jesus. This was the available Christian theology: Christ. It would be decades before a moment like this would be permanently documented. That moment on that hillside was enough. Jesus' closest disciples, most of whom were raised in the Hebrew faith, would have shared with him a knowledge of the Torah, the first five books of the Bible. This was the only framework of their religious worldview or their reference point for his teaching, but in the rabbinic tradition even this was built on a conversational wrestling with the words and their application to daily life, not some rigid, mathematical formula. And as Jesus delivers his new kingdom manifesto (which we now know as the Sermon on the Mount, Matt. 5–7), he spends a great portion of it reframing the very tradition itself, challenging and deepening all they know about it, stretching whatever the God box looked like for them. "You have heard that it was said, 'An eye for an eye and a tooth for a tooth.' But I say . . ." Over and over, Jesus gives his hearers a fresh lens through which to view faith and a higher calling rooted in the response of their lives to the love of God.

Jesus certainly had deep convictions. He was as principled as they come, but those principles were never more treasured or tightly held than the people in front of him. It isn't that virtues and ideals and standards didn't exist for him, but he never let those things obscure the humanity that crossed his path and the journey they traveled to get there. Compassion and knowledge of the other were always the driver. Jesus speaks with the Samaritan woman at the well of her need. He meets Nicodemus, the Pharisee who comes to him under the cover of night to wrestle with his questions. He praises the faith of the occupation Roman solider. He stays in the home of Zacchaeus, a despised tax collector (John 4:1–42; 3:1–21; Matt. 8:5–13; Luke 19:1–10). These weren't social constructs; they weren't representatives of hot-button issues; they weren't lazy stereotypes; they weren't religious talking points. Most of all, they weren't opportunities to debate theological systems. These were personal stories of individual souls fashioned in the image of God, and *this* is how Jesus responded to them. He didn't burden them with doctrine or allow their beliefs to keep them at a distance. He saw them. He offered them the gift of proximity and the invitation to communion. His sermons were never given in a vacuum, but always connected to a life that echoed it. This is the path to holding onto and sharing our faith convictions in the bigger table: we simply live those convictions, not requiring another to share them. We don't use our theology as a weapon; we allow it to mold us into people who really see people.

At the first student event at our church in Charlotte, I remember meeting Tracy. She and her brother were among the hundred or so middle and high school students who funneled into our converted-storefront student center that Sunday afternoon. The facility itself was off-the-charts amazing, with a massive game room, a full concession stand, and a stage area with all the bells and whistles. We'd done tons of work to get the building and our massive team of volunteers ready for the event, and I really wanted it to be amazing—and it was. I can remember ping-ponging all around the student center, introducing myself to parents, stopping to answer questions from volunteers, and working the room like a maître d' during the dinner rush. In the middle of the dizzying bombast of the moment, I happened to catch a glimpse of Tracy out of the corner of my eye. She and her older brother Caleb were standing at the edge of the room away from the crowd, both looking uncomfortable. I made my way over, introduced myself, and tried to engage them in some small talk—I got little response. I attempted a few of my go-to cheesy Youth Pastor jokes. *Nothing.* I talked to them about some fun stuff we had planned and let them know that I looked forward to getting to know them over the coming year. *Barely a smile.* I thanked them for coming and continued on, feeling a bit defeated.

Overall the rest of the night went beautifully, and the beginning of my tenure there at the church began as well as I could have hoped—but it would get even better a few days later when I received an e-mail. It was from Tracy. She began by saying that I probably wouldn't remember her (though I had) and she recounted her version of the conversation we'd had that Sunday. She went on to share some of the difficulties she'd had in the past, some of the bad choices she'd made, and the reputation she'd made for herself in school and at church. She recounted the coldness and judgment she'd received from pastors and students before. These things had all left her feeling completely uncomfortable in church, and in fact she'd been forced to be there that Sunday, as a sort of punishment by her parents. Tracy said she wanted to thank me for the time I took to speak with her and to let me know what a difference it made. I'll never forget the words she wrote to me: "I wanted to thank you. People usually don't notice me or they pretend not to see me. You made me feel *visible*." I learned so much from that e-mail and from those words. Tracy didn't need my theology or doctrine that afternoon. She needed my presence. She needed me to be available and to see her. I wish more religious people were as good at seeing people as they are at preaching at them.

With the benefit of hindsight, with two thousand years of church history, and with a billion or so books on the subject, it's tempting now to fly over the ministry of Jesus at thirty thousand feet and create some tidy, well-organized theological system, to say "Jesus clearly was referring to _____ here" or "This is how we exegete this phrase." But those living alongside Jesus didn't have this. His disciples, those entrusted to record and replicate his message for humanity, had only their shared experience to draw from and the Hebrew Scriptures as a touchstone. They had only what they saw, heard, and walked through together as a filter to understand him and to decide what God was trying to say to the world. This all underscores the reality that Jesus was far more relational then he was theological. His guests at the table, the people he encountered on the hillsides and in the streets, and his disciples didn't have seminary classes or podcasts or volumes of commentaries and mountains of resources. They had that brief moment in the history of the planet to share space and time with Jesus. They had the words he spoke to them, the parables he shared, the compassion he provided, the wounds he healed. That was their daily bread.

Maybe we don't need (and never needed) to create an elaborate, extensively footnoted religious system as a way of knowing and teaching others about the character of God. This obviously wasn't a primary or even peripheral objective of Jesus, otherwise he would have done it. He would have written everything down first and spent the three years of his public ministry doing nothing but lecturing people on the right things to believe and how to get to heaven. He would have handed out tracts and given altar calls and moved on—but he didn't. Yes, he preached, he taught, he healed—*and* he lived. This is one of the clearest and yet most neglected lessons of the Gospels: life as theology. Jesus gives us the perfect blueprint of a captivating apologetic of love that, were we to choose it, might bring the greatest revival the planet has ever seen.

This is the very heart of the bigger table. It isn't about formulating and defending some ironclad religious system that we proof-text and memorize and attempt to convince others to adopt. It's not about winning theological discussions or defending worldviews. It is about tangibly living in a way that responds to what we believe about our own belovedness and about the belovedness of those we live alongside. It is about knowing and being known and trying to incarnate Jesus in our midst in the process, and trusting God with whatever happens in the wake of that. There's no battle to win, no ground to protect, no persuading to do. There is no pressure from above or within, and no pressure applied to the other. There is simply (as there was for those living with Jesus and sitting on that rugged hillside) a real-time, relational, intentional communing with others in redemptive community.

You may think I'm saying that your theological beliefs don't matter, that deep spiritual convictions don't matter; that this is all just some feel-good, Kum-ba-ya, summer-camp religion where anything goes. Well, it is and it isn't. The idea isn't to abandon your personal convictions, but it also isn't to demand that anyone else share them in order to be in deep, meaningful fellowship with you. If your theology isn't connected directly and visibly to your daily living and if it doesn't saturate the relationships you engage in, then it's merely theory: noble, beautiful, powerful theory, but theory just the same. The table is the practice of living theologically, of simply embodying one's beliefs rather than leading with them, which is a dying art form. Over the past two thousand years the world has had far more than its fill of theoretical followers of Jesus, who believe the right things, say the right things, and live lives nearly devoid of anything remotely resembling him. People have seen far too few incarnational livers of his clear apologetic of love. The former is the heart of a now dying religious institution growing more and more irrelevant to the world. The latter is the hope of our faith. It is the Church that will be and must be if it is to remain. It's also a messy proposition.

A couple years ago, my wife and I were invited to a local LGBTQ foundation's yearly gala. It was a chance to support the wonderful work they were doing here in North Carolina, to celebrate the recent national marriage-equality legislation (and to get dressed up and have dinner in a place where the place mats didn't also substitute as coloring books). We parked the car and made our way toward the beautiful center-city venue a few blocks away. As we walked, a noise began to steadily rise above that of the regular street traffic, growing louder and louder until it fully enveloped the street. Closer to the theater we could see a group of bullhorn-wielding, sign-carrying street preachers, shouting Scriptures at passersby, warning people of hell, and screaming pointed, distorted prayers through distorted portable speakers. These folks were countered on the opposite side of the street by a larger, more colorful, more exuberant crowd holding whimsical signs, shaking rainbow-colored tambourines, and providing sarcastic verbal counterpunches to the preachers' dour, brimstone warnings. We walked through the center of that tempest of volleying noise and into the event, and as the door closed behind us it was silenced.

Once inside we laughed a bit at first at the sheer spectacle of it all, and the poorly chosen battle of the outgunned and outnumbered preachers. But later we realized what a tragedy we'd witnessed and just how clearly it illustrated what the Church becomes when it puts theology at its center: two groups of people yelling from a distance, one attacking and the other defending, but neither being heard, neither being known, neither's humanity allowed to be visible between the taunts and verbal jousts. These were no longer uniquely designed individuals in a shared journey, but anonymous soldiers on either side of a holy war. It was a battle of belief systems with no account for those

in the trenches. And the most regretful thing about it all is that
Christians should be different. When it comes to other people,
even those we may disagree with, we should know better and
do better. We have an example. We have the table of Christ as
the template for how to see people and to acknowledge their
inherent value.

We have in Jesus the greatest model of compassion and
kindness ever to walk the planet, and that needs to count for
something. It needs to influence how we as followers of Christ
interact with people we disagree with, or we end up simply
being clanging cymbals, a loud, loveless noise in the ears of
those around us, and feeling justified in doing so. We need to
figure out how to live without the bullhorn and to find that
quiet place of civility that Jesus finds so many times with so
many different people. The idea of universal family or kinship
is at the core of the Christian faith too, of all people made in
the image of God, all creations of the same Creator, all equally
flawed, all equally worthy of compassion. Our story is that
every person is the neighbor we are called to love as ourselves.

The beauty of the bigger table is that it creates proximity
in the way Jesus did. It destroys distance between people, and
distance—whether real or imagined—is the enemy of relationship. This chasm allows us to *otherize* people with little accountability to their reality. It enables us to hold onto the belief that
the crudely drawn caricatures we fashion for those we disagree
with are at all accurate, allowing us to craft a clearly defined
us-vs.-them narrative and place them opposite us. This simple
narrative can't accommodate people's individual stories, as this
is too labor intensive and time consuming. Instead it lumps
those stories together into the closest-fitting generalization (a
political party, a religious tradition, a people-group stereotype)
and operates with that as truth. But these containers are simply
never adequate. Our labels are never large enough for unique
image bearers of God, and unless we become relentless in really
straining to see individual people, we will always default to this
easy, lazy shorthand, and we will always shortchange the beauty
within them. We'll also be satisfied viewing them from this safe

distance of our self-righteousness and shouting through bull-horns or shaking tambourines.

The kind of intimacy Jesus shares with people, the kind that was and is transformational, only comes with close proximity. It is not possible screamed from across the road or shouted from a pulpit or laid out in a carefully researched dissertation. It cannot be gleaned from a clever meme or a spirited Twitter exchange or a hermeneutic debate. It only comes through the redemptive relationship forged when we are willing to sit across from people who believe differently than we believe, willing to get close enough and stay long enough to see both their unique humanity and their inherent divinity. This is how we love people well; it is how we put flesh on our faith; and it is how we follow so close behind the rabbi Jesus that we are covered in his dust. The only way the table can really expand is when we, like Christ, are willing to take our place across from those who appear to be or even desire to be our adversaries. Jesus' call to embrace *love as theology* isn't merely a surface, sugary platitude. It's the most difficult, radical, time-consuming work of reflecting Christ to the world around us. In the end, the thing that glorifies God isn't our belief system, but how we treat those who don't share that belief system. We can be people of deep conviction without needing to pick up a bullhorn.

13

Pharisees, Heresies, and Least-Lovers

I want you to think about your eyes for a moment. I want you to think about the way you see the world, especially if you're a person of faith. When you encounter war, poverty, violence, addiction, human trafficking, and all the other things that horrify you, what story do you tell yourself? Usually we fall into one of two camps. Some Christians look at the dysfunction, injustice, and discord around them as sure signs of a fallen creation: proof of a sinful, rebellious culture rejecting God and paying the price. They see suffering as the by-product of wickedness, the unpleasantness they rub shoulders with every day clear symptoms of the moral decay of everything. These followers of Jesus primarily see *sin*, and that sin is the lens through which they view the world around them and the people in their path. With this as their primary filter, they tend to respond with a burden to save souls. The answer to everything becomes conversion, salvation as eternal rescue from the cancer that afflicts us all. It is all *next-life* focused. Or they see Jesus as an instant, magic cure-all for the behavior in others that they find objectionable or uncomfortable. They imagine that simply "coming to Jesus" will eliminate all the immorality that may or may not bother Jesus—but that certainly bothers them. Apparently they've come across more fully perfected Christians than I have.

Other followers of Jesus see something different when they look at the mess in front of them. They see pain. They see need. They see longing. They see an opportunity to bring restoration here and now. They are focused as much on *this world* as they are on the next. These, I'll contend, are the eyes of Christ, and these are the eyes of those who would build the bigger table. We are learning to see differently than we once did.

In the ninth chapter of the Gospel of Matthew, Jesus looks upon the crowd gathered before him and is deeply burdened by what he sees, not because of what they are doing or not doing, but because of what is being done *to* them and what it is creating *in* them (9:35–38). He is moved in that moment, not by some moral defect but by their internal turmoil. Just as when he feeds the multitudes, Jesus is not concerned with behavior modification, as we so often imagine; he is most concerned with meeting the needs that prevent people from knowing their belovedness, and he offers an expression of God's provision. Matthew records that Jesus, seeing those in front of him, notes not their conduct but their condition, observing that they are "harassed and helpless, like sheep without a shepherd." This realization prompts a passionate, public appeal for those who would do the work of restoration and healing in the name of God. The distinction between seeing *sin* and seeing *suffering* is revelatory if we really let it seep into the deepest hollows of our hearts. Jesus' default response to the fragile humanity before him is not contempt but compassion.

This is often the primary difference between him and so many of those of us who follow him. When we encounter the many ills of the world, we find ourselves growing more and more callous toward people, more and more judgmental, less and less hopeful. Rather than seeing the hurting humanity we encounter every day as an opportunity to be the very loving presence of Jesus, we see them as reason to withdraw from it all. Faith becomes about retreating from the world when it should be about moving toward it. As we walk deeper into organized religion, we run the risk of eventually becoming fully blind to the tangible suffering around us, less concerned about mending wounds or changing systems, and more preoccupied with saving or condemning souls.

In this way, the spiritual eyes through which we see the world change everything. If our default lens is sin, we tend to look ahead to the afterlife, but if we focus on suffering, we'll lean toward presently transforming the planet in real time—and we'll create community accordingly. The former seeks to help people escape the encroaching moral decay by getting them into heaven; the latter takes seriously the prayer Jesus teaches his disciples, that they would make the kingdom come—that through lives resembling Christ and work that perpetuates his work, we would actually bring heaven down. Practically speaking, sin management seems easier because essentially all that is required of us is to preach, to call out people's errors and invite them to repentance, and to feel we've been faithful. But seeing suffering requires us to step into the broken, jagged chaos of people's lives to be agents of healing and change. It's far more time consuming and much more difficult to do as a faith community. It is a lot easier to train preachers to lead people in a Sinner's Prayer than it is to equip them to address the systematic injustices around them.

Earlier we talked about the emotional distance that enables us to retain our stereotypes and biases about people, allowing our prejudices to go unchallenged and misperceptions to remain uncorrected. When I had that safe distance growing up, I believed all the false stories I'd inherited about the LGBTQ community, about people of color, about Muslims, because I didn't have the instructive closeness to correct me. I could develop my own narrative about who they were, what they were like, how they lived, what they believed. Whatever broad brush I wanted to paint them with was fine, and consequently I held a distorted view of large swaths of humanity. But this distance we put between others and ourselves has another consequence on our spiritual journeys: it mistakenly inflates our own moral

worth, elevating us in our minds above other people based on
what we think we know about them.

The Pharisees lived like this. They tend to get a bad rap,
usually serving as the convenient foils of our Sunday sermons
and Bible studies, easily identifiable black-hatted villains to
serve as examples of hypocrisy and hubris. And while it's true
that Jesus saves his most pointed words and harshest critiques
for them, they weren't as one-dimensional as we imagine them
to be. These were deeply religious, extremely faithful men
wanting to please and honor God and to preserve the faith of
their fathers in a world that threatened it. The problem was
that their desire to place a hedge of protection around godli-
ness and to preserve tradition had become toxic, segregating
them from the growing number of people they began to deem
morally inferior. When you place yourself in the position of
defending the faith, you begin to believe you have cornered the
market on piety and truth. The entire world outside of their
religious bubble seemed like a threat. They grew ever more
insulated from a humanity they resented, and because of this
the poor and marginalized now merited only their contempt,
never their compassion. Though they were incredibly earnest
and God fearing, they grew more and more oblivious to the
suffering around them and to their responsibility to step into
that hurt and bring life. They lived as walking contradictions
of love for God and disregard for so many of God's people.
Religion had become a mechanism for separating themselves
from people, and they grew hardened toward the suffering they
endured, convinced that it was deserved.

This is why you see Jesus so incensed at the religious leaders, because their vision had been so distorted that they'd
lost the plot and their purpose. In the twenty-third chapter
of Matthew's biography of Jesus, the author relays a scathing,
relentless scolding of these professed men of God, calling them
hypocrites and blind guides, and taking them to task for misleading those entrusted to them. Even though they knew the
Scriptures and were educated and believed their cause righteous, they completely missed Jesus in their midst. In theory

they were on the same side as him, but their living testimony couldn't have been more different. Though seeking to glorify the same God, they and Jesus looked nothing alike. Interesting how easily that can happen. Ask most people outside of the Church what they think of when they hear the word *Christian*, and you get a description that looks a lot more like the Pharisees than the rabbi Jesus.

This hardness and victim blaming is symptomatic of so much of the Church in America today, where we see religious people who are generous with judgment and stingy with grace. Our affinity-based faith communities can have the same effect on us today as the cloistered self-righteous religion of the Pharisees. In the comfortable confines of people who agree with us and look like us and believe what we believe, we can rationalize the reasons for the suffering in the world and our reasons for not intervening: the poor are poor because they are lazy, addicts are addicted because they are weak, gay people are gay because they've chosen to reject God. Whatever pain they're going through is of their own design. Our hearts grow similarly calloused, and our eyes, much like the Pharisees', become attuned more toward moral judgment. We need to pay attention to that if we're going to expand the table, because those are the people we'll be trying to earn an audience with. Theirs are the extra chairs we're looking to add. Our "fend for yourself," "pull yourself up by your own bootstraps," "every person for themselves" version of Christianity is a far cry from the Jesus who washed feet, fed multitudes, healed wounds, comforted grievers. It all comes back to the eyes you use when you look at the crowds, whether across the world, online—or right in front of you.

I nearly ruined a promising relationship because I was seeing with judgmental, callous eyes. Ace was in his late teens, and he'd been attending our student ministry for a couple of weeks as the guest of some of our regulars. The cluster of teenagers he'd been hanging with had grown increasingly loud and disruptive, and one Sunday it all came to a head, eventually leading to a heated confrontation in the parking lot between these students and myself, along with another adult leader. Ace spoke up in defense of the group, and he challenged me on mistreating them. I'm embarrassed to say that I handled this moment really badly. Ace and his friends were all young men of color, and without realizing it I'd allowed my older false stories to creep in just enough to convince me that I was right, just enough to thin my patience down to nothing, just enough to stop listening. I dug in and doubled down, even as I knew I was wrong. (Pride will tend to do that.) The conversation became less heated and finally petered out. Ace and his friends left that afternoon, and I was fairly certain I wouldn't see him again, but fortunately he's a much better follower of Jesus and human being than I am. He showed up a week later for Sunday services. I asked if we could talk, and he graciously agreed. I learned that Ace was traveling on his own for two hours by public buses just to reach our suburban church, that he had an extremely difficult home life and was finding something he lacked in our community—and I'd been a lousy host and an even worse representative of Jesus. I began driving Ace home and we became really good friends. Eventually he started working with our elementary school kids, and he's as good as it gets. I've met few people as naturally wired to encourage and care for people, and the students adore him. I nearly missed really seeing Ace that Sunday afternoon because my false stories had clouded my vision. I am grateful that he was gracious enough to give me another chance, and that I didn't blow it. He's still doing beautiful work in the lives of young people in Charlotte, and I'm proud to be considered a friend.

"What do you talk about at dinner with former prostitutes?" I wondered to myself, and then asked out loud to my wife as we drew closer to our favorite Uptown Charlotte restaurant, where we had dinner reservations. We would be two of a party of eight, including my pastor and his wife, three young women who'd recently been rescued from the commercial sex trade, and a member of the local advocacy group our church had recently partnered with. My pastor had just texted me to tell me that he was running late and that we'd be on our own for a bit. "Perfect," I thought to myself, my hands quickly pooling with sweat. I pulled the car into the parking garage and tried to prepare myself to carry a conversation I was certain was destined to be both awkward and depressing. I'd be repenting greatly of that fear in a matter of minutes. The bigger table has a way of surprising and humbling you like that.

Within a few seconds of meeting these bright, funny, sweet young women, I felt at home. We spent the next two hours talking comfort food and faith and family. We compared our favorite Prince songs and laughed like old friends. It was as sweet a time as I'd ever had around a table, and I was sorry to see it end.

The road to this unlikely but redemptive meal began nearly two years earlier. Like many churches, we'd just started to understand the depth and scope of the human trafficking crisis. After seeing International Justice Mission (IJM) founder Gary Hagen speak at a conference in Atlanta, we were incredibly moved by the work they were doing to rescue children out of the commercial sex trade and began talking about how we might partner with them. We decided to create a Christmas sermon series, culminating in a Christmas Eve offering devoted solely to IJM. We were blown away by the response of our people, who provided the largest one-time day of giving in our church's history to that point, and we celebrated being able to provide IJM with tangible assistance, knowing it would enable girls halfway across the world whose names we'd never know to have the freedom they so deserved. Those few weeks had awakened our people and whet our appetites to do something greater. The table of our compassion was expanding exponentially, and we were seeing the kind of movement of God that cannot be denied, forecast, or managed.

North Carolina is, unfortunately, one of the hubs of human trafficking in the United States. As we headed into the new year, we decided as a staff to do something that would have a local impact. We began connecting with Charlotte-area ministries working to care for victims of the sex trade and searched for a partner to do something beautiful together. Once we met the people at On Eagle's Wings (OEW), we knew we'd found that partner. OEW houses girls who have been rescued from forced prostitution and holistically cares for them with counseling, education, life skills, and spiritual support, and in general loves them as they deserve to be loved, preparing them for a life beyond the kind they'd known and endured.

We conceived a four-week sermon series called Home, with the end goal of giving OEW a debt-free house and supporting their continued work in our city. Those four weeks were as emotional and galvanizing as any we'd ever experienced. That final Sunday, our people again exceeded our every expectation, as we were able to find, refurbish, and give a new home to OEW, and the deed along with it. It was the Church being the very best of itself, and it's a day I'll never forget, yet not half as memorable as that dinner two years later, where I had another false story rewritten.

It was that long, meandering journey of learning and listening, of praying and asking, of dreaming and doing that set the table for our unlikely meal that day in Uptown Charlotte. It would have never happened had we not done the slow, arduous work of seeing suffering and responding. We didn't allow our people safe distance to be the Pharisee, but gave them proximity to hurting people and asked them to respond. But more than that, we asked our community not to see these women as somehow lesser and needing to be saved, but as equals needing us to stand with them. We tried to give our people new eyes. Building a bigger table means trying to see people beyond their circumstances. And there on that Saturday afternoon twenty-four months later we gathered, passing biscuits and sharing stories, not as ministers and former prostitutes, but as equally flawed brothers and sisters seated around the table sharing life together. There was no separation between us, and no elevation of one above the other. There was no judgment and no condemnation and no earning of fellowship. There was simply love in abundance.

This is the place Jesus invites us to, regardless of who we imagine seated there. It is the Church he calls us to create: the kind that sees humanity and need first, the kind that leads with compassion. There's no way the people in our church will ever see human trafficking the same way again, and I'll never understand prostitution the same way. I'll remember that there are stories there, and that my faith calls me to learn and treasure those stories and the people who own them. I'll never again be able to dismiss someone based on the label the world affixes to them.

This is what the table gives us when it expands around us—an unrelenting desire to love our neighbor, the realization that every person *is* that neighbor, and the wisdom to abandon any illusion that we are more deserving of dining with Jesus than another. It removes the Pharisee in us and causes us to see the hurting places we are called to bring healing to, and we move. As you look at the crowds before you, check your eyes.

14

The Church Will Be Queer[*]

The early Church was a historic underdog of biblical proportions. It had absolutely no business surviving. In the wake of Jesus leaving, it existed in the vise-like squeeze between the Roman government and local Jewish leadership, both of whom deemed it a threat or a problem. They were a people without a home. The remaining movement of only a few hundred faithful should have fizzled and died out with Christ's departure, as it didn't seem to have much else going for it. It didn't have power or political sway or any of the tangible markers we use to identify success. No financial support, no building, no cultural influence. Two thousand years later, we shouldn't even have a Church to critique or defend at all, and the fact that we do speaks eloquently to what it was in those first weeks and months, what it's become since, and how far we have drifted since then in both message and methodology. The book of Acts documents that as the followers of Jesus lived in loving interdependence—as Jew and Gentile, man and woman, slave and free, respected and reviled all came together in mutual

[*]**queer** *adj.* odd, peculiar, different, strange

respect—the Church grew exponentially (2:42–47). Despite adverse conditions, they began making a name for themselves in the incredibly hostile world they were born into.

Most people don't realize that followers of Jesus didn't coin the term *Christian*. There were no creative team meetings to talk brand strategy, logo design, and market saturation. There were no promotional campaigns or demographic studies. They simply had each other and their living testimony together—and it was all they needed. The label of "Little Christs" was created for them and affixed to them by those outside their tiny but growing community, and it wasn't exactly a compliment, but simply a way to identify them. Yet as people watched how they lived, how they faithfully cared for one another, how they embraced diversity, how they lifted one another up, they noticed that they resembled Jesus. The believers began to claim ownership of the name *Christian* and to redefine the word and themselves, precisely because of their bigger table.

This was far more radical than we can really appreciate today. In a culture reinforcing the sharply drawn lines between people—the lines of religion, ethnicity, nationality, and gender—the followers of Jesus were erasing the lines, knocking down walls, and pulling up chairs. The incredibly narrow "chosen people" of the Old Testament tradition was now giving way to a far more expansive new "kingdom people" based solely on their faith in Jesus. As the apostle Paul would describe, in their tribe, there were no longer any divisions that mattered more than what grafted them together in redemptive community (Gal. 3:26–29). They were one body with disparate but equally necessary members. Their primary commonality was Christ. He became their peace. To be *Christian* meant to willingly cast aside any idea that another was unworthy to share in fellowship; it was to give up the moral evaluations and preconceptions they may have had before. When we look back at the table of Jesus, this early Christian community really shouldn't surprise us because he was pointing toward this day the entire time, as he met with lepers and Pharisees and tax collectors and street people. The early Church wasn't doing anything in its infancy other than replicating his life together with those in their midst. In the two thousand years since then, we've added a great deal around this idea, cumbersome layers of tradition and doctrine and pageantry, and yet these are the things we could easily discard and still have the essence of the Church. We would still have people sharing life.

Reclaiming a derogatory term the way the early Christians did is something the LGBTQ community understands well. One of my favorite episodes of *The Simpsons* illustrates it succinctly. It features director John Waters, who voices a character named John, a gay man befriended (after much objection) by Homer Simpson. During one of Homer's many homophobic tirades early in the episode, he struggles to find the right word to describe John and those like him, to which John interjects, "Queer?" Homer is incensed. "And that's another thing!" he screams incredulously. "That's *our* word for making fun of *you*. We *need* it!" Younger generations of the LGBTQ community have commandeered the word *queer* as a fitting definition of their uniqueness. For many, what was once a slur has been transformed into a declaration of beautiful difference, and Christians should affirm when this happens for marginalized communities. We should remember where we came from and that we were born out of scorn and ridicule, and that we are supposed to be the people of the mischaracterized underdog.

Luke's document of the early Church is a reminder that when God's Spirit is present, walls and barriers become irrelevant. When people are fully gripped with a love that imitates Christ, whatever differences exist don't have to fall away; they simply yield to the shared purpose of caring for the other as one's own. We don't lose our distinctiveness when we come together at the table of Jesus, but we understand that there is a greater unity holding it all together. This is what should distinguish us from other gatherings. When Jesus began the new kingdom movement, it had only its beautiful oddness, its counterintuitive compassion, its wonderful *different-ness* to do the work of drawing people to it. This was its sole calling card. The early Christians were a queer lot for sure, and this is the very reason they were not extinguished as they began. There were a number of professed messiahs with cults of personality walking around in those days, and when those leaders died, their movements died with them. Christ's people were strange enough to persevere, and it makes little sense.

Today the Church in America is ubiquitous. It is in danger of becoming indistinguishable from the surrounding culture, and as a result it is also in danger of becoming extinct. It is Egypt. It is Babylon. It is Rome. The Church in so many ways has morphed into the very bloated, opulent, materialistic *culture* that Jesus calls us to live counter to. It has lost the beautiful oddness that made it so alluring to begin with, and as a result church leaders spend so much time trying to figure out how to package and market Christianity to make it more appealing. Ironically, these efforts tend to make the church even *more* like the surrounding culture. Our worship services mimic entertainment, our facilities replicate coffee shops and conference centers, our organizations mirror corporate America, our leaders cosplay celebrity. It's all become a variation on the theme. So many of the things that made the people of Jesus so decidedly strange in those early days are gone.

We no longer earn the name *Christian* from those standing outside and looking at us. They don't see us living together in Christlikeness, or being the most diverse gathering on the planet, or all people finding their inherent worth there and feeling compelled to invite the world in. So often when they look at us, instead of seeing Little Christs, they see very little Christ. In fact, the term *Christian* is now so loaded with baggage and collateral damage that we're all straining to distance ourselves from it for fear of losing our audience with people. There is very little about organized Christianity that really resembles Jesus right now, and the answer isn't to chase more of the same. The answer isn't to double down on wall building or separation or pharisaical stone throwing. It isn't (as some conservative segments are doing) to ratchet up the rhetoric and to raise the volume and to broker in fear. The answer also isn't to get slicker and more media savvy and more culturally relevant. The Church is not going to suddenly thrive in the days ahead because it has gorgeous facilities and charismatic leaders. It already has such things in abundance. It is going to thrive when it again chooses to live in radical opposition to the barriers between people. The bad news is that organized Christianity as we know it is certainly dying, but the good news is that what began in the early Church won't die with it. And the *really* good news is that we don't need to reinvent Christian community; we only have to reach back and retrieve it. We only have to begin the simple, small, slow work of coming to the table and investing time in one another.

The people of Jesus will never again have the exponential growth nor the cultural impact we once had until we become welcoming to the whole of humanity again. And make no mistake, this diversity and openness and welcome of difference all come with a price. In his letter to the Christian community gathered in Galatia, the apostle Paul recalls the deep schism there regarding the acceptance of Gentiles into what had to this point been predominantly a Jewish religious movement. Paul openly confronts Peter, one of Jesus' initial twelve disciples, for caving in to the pressure of the powerful Jewish faction demanding that Gentiles be circumcised before being welcomed into the Christian community. He accuses Peter of withdrawing from the non-Jews and misleading those who looked to him as a leader and mentor. Two powerful figures of a fledgling community, both with devoted supporters, engaged in heated debate on matters of inclusion. This couldn't have been comfortable or easy, and yet it was the cost of forging a way forward. We should never be fooled into believing that conflict will not be present as we seek the bigger table; in fact, we should welcome that conflict, because it is a requirement when movement takes place. Yes, the early Church was beautiful, but it was a beautiful mess, one that probably felt decidedly less rosy than it appears to us from here. When James tells us to rejoice in our "trials" (Jas. 1:2), he certainly includes those that are self-inflicted.

The only thing we really have to offer the world right now is all we've ever really had to offer it: a shared expression of lives that reflect the life of Jesus. That is the still the greatest thing we can aspire to and the best chance we have to alter the planet in the way those first Little Christs did. Modern evangelical theology (using the eyes that see primarily sin) tends to rightly emphasize the Church as set apart and distinct, but it usually uses the wrong measurements to assess its success in the matter. It forgets that the set-apart-ness of the earliest Christians wasn't about doctrinal purity or some saved/lost, in/out, righteous/wicked divide—it was about interdependency and diversity. In the second chapter of the book of Acts, Luke describes those early believers gathering to recall Jesus' lessons to them, being in daily community, sharing meals, praying together. He describes their pooling of possessions and their providing for the needs of one another and their public displays of fellowship—and he makes a direct correlation between these things and the response of those outside their community. Luke writes that people are "being saved" as they encounter this redemptive community. That powerful, visible expression of the barrier-breaking love of God by the community of professed believers is the light shining before men that Jesus spoke of, describing the "good works" they would do together being a reminder of God (Matt. 5:16). The body of Christ today is not this sacred kind of different when it withdraws from the world or when it emulates corporate America or when it mirrors a political party or when it adopts the trappings of pop culture; it is such when (as two thousand years earlier) it clearly and quietly manifests the character of Christ. That is the plan. That is the agenda. That is the strategy. It isn't about taking some loud, blustery stand against sin, it isn't about how much we pound our pulpits or how loudly we condemn or the cultural battles we wage. It isn't about drawing some moral line in the sand. It's about our willingness to be with people and live alongside them.

This is why the inclusion of the LGBTQ community into the body of Christ is so important in these days, and why it is one of the hills worth dying on for me as a pastor, because it is one of the greatest opportunities we have to set the kind of table Jesus set for the believers he entrusted to carry the message forward. It is an opportunity to show the watching world what Christ looks like by emulating him. The Church's resistance to and persecution of gay, lesbian, bisexual, transgender, and questioning men and women is a push against the Holy Spirit because it runs in direct opposition to the heart of Jesus as reflected in the Gospel biographies and the book of Acts. It isn't just shrinking the table: it's walling off the table from those who desire to be present. And the answer isn't offering some tentative, heavily conditioned token tolerance as a compromise. (If that were the case, Jesus' table gatherings would have been very different.) It is to be fully obedient to Jesus' command to love another as oneself. The straight Church doesn't need to tolerate or pacify or throw scraps to the Christian LGBTQ community, it needs the LGBTQ community for the same reason it needs all those seeking and walking in faith regardless of their gender or skin color or sexual orientation—because these folks are breathing sanctuaries of the Spirit of God and because without them any version of the Church is still inferior and incomplete. Until the queer Christian community is received fully and welcomed and included without caveat or restraint by the institutional Church, the Church will continue to be less grace-filled, less rich in its complexity, and less in the image of Christ than it should be. When Christians attempt to exclude any group from the table, they distort the Church because they deny the heart of Jesus for all of humanity. Discrimination hinders people from finding community, and it robs the Church of the tremendous gifts that diversity brings.

Years ago I hired two openly gay people to serve in student ministry with me, and throughout our time together, their sexual orientation never once served as a barrier to their ability to care for our teens or to share the love of God with them. On the contrary, they had compassion and tenderness that only comes from experiencing so much hurt and from overcoming so much just to get to Jesus. They were some of the greatest table setters I've ever worked alongside. Our community was richer and better because of their presence, and that's simply not something you can argue or exegete me out of, because I've lived it.

When it comes to removing barriers between people or between people and God, we as the body of Christ should be on the very front lines. We should be leading the charge. We should be defining the movement of equality and justice, not bringing up the rear and definitely not digging in our heels and fighting against it with all that we have. That simply doesn't glorify God, and it isn't making disciples either. The world is seeing this and rejecting it. I hear their stories every single day. The name *Christian* is no longer synonymous with Jesus out in the world, but with bigotry, with power, with discrimination. *This* is the script that we who desire the bigger table must flip.

And once you begin to look at the world through the eyes of compassion, you'll notice the places where diversity is not welcome; you'll see the people who are invisible to others; you'll find the sweet spot where you feel led to begin expanding the table. You may find affinity toward a very specific community, marginalized because of their skin color, religion, sexual orientation, income level, or other characteristics, and move intentionally toward that community (as happened with me originally), or you may simply seek a broader idea of unity where you are and look to create that in your community or church. Either way, the act of expanding the table is itself a teacher. You will be led by it to stories you'd never heard, to need you never were aware of, and to ministry that has yet to be created. You will be led to a better version of yourself too.

Our church here in Raleigh is . . . weird; there's no other way to say it. Our theology is purposefully nebulous, our doctrine not clearly delineated. Our services are humble, rather rough-around-the-edges affairs. We are unapologetically both Christian and fully open to people of all faiths, and we don't believe this to be at all oxymoronic. We are fully affirming of the LGBTQ community. We celebrate theological dissonance. We welcome differing understandings of the Bible. Our community is also a church with a far bigger table than almost any I've ever visited or been a part of. When people arrive for the first time, they are surprised to find that there are no boxes to check, no hoops to jump through, no impressions to make—there is simply welcome. Our community is unpredictable and unorganized and decidedly messy in the most beautiful of ways. The first time our family visited this church was just after I'd been "released" from my previous church, and we were all reeling. The minister, Doug, gave a profoundly moving message about the danger of otherizing people in the wake of the racial unrest in Baltimore. Then he followed up with the question, "So, what are you thinking?" I quickly realized it wasn't rhetorical. He was waiting for responses. Hands went up all around us and people began speaking: affirming things Doug had just said, pushing back against others, asking their own questions to the community and taking responses. People laughed, some got angry, a few cried. It was extraordinary to hear some of the greatest insight, some of the best "preaching," from those sitting next to us. The same things happened the next Sunday. Turns out it happens here every Sunday. And this is one of the ways our community is seeking to be what the Church was when it was weird to the world, by making sure everyone's voice is valued and heard.

The expanding of the table isn't an effort to abandon our Christianity or to reject the Church. It's an attempt to jettison everything else but that which is essential to reflecting Jesus in the world and to sharing in redemptive community with people in a way that is so loving, so embracing, and so open, that it seems *queer* to the rest of the world. And that will be what brings revolution.

15

Mama Bear Hugs and Mama Dragon Fire

My kids have superpowers. Well, at least one specific and fairly annoying one. They're able to discern from any part of the house or surrounding area when I have chocolate in my personal possession. No matter how quiet I am or how carefully I've concealed it or how covertly I uncover it, the moment that silver foil begins to tear it sends some invisible tremors through the air that only the hairs of their inner ears can detect—and as if by teleportation, they appear. And not only them, but a small army of neighborhood kids, all surrounding me like starved, cocoa-crazed zombies.

Good things have a way of attracting people. Radical hospitality. Full authenticity. True diversity. Agenda-free community. These things are holy multipliers. They have a beautiful way of replicating themselves, of creating their own momentum. We see this in the documenting of the early Church, and this has been our experience at North Raleigh Community Church as we've begun to do this work of creating redemptive community in person and online: You expand the table, and it expands more. You stretch to more fully reflect the character of Jesus, and you are stretched further. You move to follow God's leading, and you are nudged beyond the place you chose to land. When the table expands, you find yourself sitting across from people you'd never have found any other way.

But the bigger table also has a way of attracting those upset by this kind of grace-filled community.

I'm not quite sure what heaven and hell will be like, but I'm fairly certain that I got a good glimpse of each of them in my e-mail in-box on September 20, 2014. Three days earlier I'd published a blog post called "If I Have Gay Children: Four Promises from a Christian Pastor/Parent."[*] It was an eleven-hundred-word preemptive love letter to my two young children, in the event that I one day find out they are LGBTQ. The piece was an effort to humanize something that Christians have dehumanized for so long, to try and move the dialogue regarding faith and sexuality from some distant, antiseptic "issue" to a close, profoundly intimate story for those reading. After nearly two decades in student ministry, seeing first-hand the incredible damage being done to so many young gay people and their families in the name of God, I felt I finally needed to speak explicitly and directly into the faith community, leveraging whatever influence I had. I wanted to write in a way that literally brought the issue of sexuality home to those who might never consider the possibility. My hope was that by framing the conversation of sexual orientation around the common and deeply personal experience of love of family, that some would approach it from a different heart place than they had before, that they might begin engaging the LGBTQ community and the topic in a new way. As the post reached a few million people, my e-mail in-box was flooded with hundreds of messages arriving each day. I soon found myself in the middle of a loud, spirited debate between disparate strangers.

We all prefer the illusion of a *clean* religious conversation, especially when it comes to those we deem morally inferior. We like to imagine that we can fire off a few Scripture quotes, trade

---

[*] John Pavlovitz, "If I Have Gay Children (Four Promises from a Christian Pastor and Parent)," *Stuff That Needs to Be Said* (blog), June 25, 2015, http://johnpavlovitz.com/2015/06/25/if-i-have-gay-children-four-promises-from-a-christian-pastor-and-parent/.

insults, and then simply step away satisfied that we've represented God and obediently confronted a "sinner." We can do such damage while fooling ourselves into believing that we've done so with no actual human toll. But here, hour after hour in my in-box, was that toll in horrible, shameful, heartbreaking detail—and I had to deal with it. I couldn't rationalize it away or pretend it wasn't real. My in-box held mountains of vile profanity and utter contempt; giant hills of crude jokes, physical violence, and white-hot fear; piles of school-hallway harassment, city-street beatdowns, church shunning, workplace hazing, brutal self-harm, and all sorts of perpetual, personal terrorism. Most of these people claimed the name of Jesus, but Jesus was not reflected or glorified in any of it, and he was not pleased by it either. There were also expressions of effusive praise from the opposite spiritual sideline, but what moved me the most were the responses to the post that I most needed and hoped to see, the ones I truly had no way of adequately preparing myself for: the ones not from the sidelines, but from those in the trenches.

Sometimes you read words and they aren't words; they're more like wounds. You can feel that those on the other side of them—rather than writing—are bleeding. The suffering and the sadness and the anger are so thick, and the depth of the pain so profound, you feel you're seeing someone on the inside. Reading the stories that began to pour in, I felt like people were tearing themselves open and letting me into the deepest places of their souls. I'd been given access to the truest truth of other human beings. It was and is holy ground, and it's why this book exists. These weren't statistics, they weren't numbers, they weren't causes, and they weren't culture-war talking points. They were brothers, daughters, uncles, mothers, best friends, bosses, coworkers, and next-door neighbors. They were flesh and blood, God-breathed lives riddled with desperate, unanswered prayers to be changed; with crippling addictions and self-harm sought as refuge; with fractured, severed relationships with treasured loved ones unable or unwilling to receive them as they were.

The massive response to the "If I Have Gay Children" post opened doors for ministry I would never have dreamed of and gave me the opportunity to pastor people whose paths I never expected to cross. I first became aware of the Mama Bears—open-minded Christian mothers of LGBTQ children—after one of my readers shared with me her personal story, and those of the now more than twelve hundred Christian moms of LGBTQ children connected in a private Facebook group called Serendipitydodah for Moms.[*] These women had been setting a bigger table long before I ever met them. They'd all experienced something that has made them family, something that transcended theology, denomination, upbringing, and even their faith traditions. They'd all found themselves living in the incredible tension between their faith tradition and their LGBTQ children—and they help one another navigate it. A month after hearing about them, I connected with the group's leader, Liz Dyer, and was invited to spend a few days as a temporary guest in the group, asking questions and hearing stories and being whatever encouragement I could be from a distance. I was blown away by their strength, the depth of their faith, and their unrelenting desire to love both God and their kids well. I asked them to share with me what they wished more Christians knew about them and about their families in a post on my blog titled "Shouting into the Wind: Words from the Hearts of Christian Moms with LGBTQ Children."[†] Here are just a few of their words to me that day:

> I would like people to know that as I prayed for God to change my son, he changed me instead. I am grateful for the work God has done and continues to do in me.

> I would want the church to know that I needed someone who shared my faith to tell me it's OK to accept my

---

[*] Serendipitydodah for Moms can be reached by contacting Liz Dyer at lizdyer55@gmail.com or at https://serendipitydodah.wordpress.com.

[†] John Pavlovitz, "Shouting into the Wind: Words from the Hearts of Christian Moms with LGBTQ Children," *Stuff That Needs to Be Said* (blog), February 15, 2015, http://johnpavlovitz .com/2015/02/15/shouting-into-the-wind-words-from-the-hearts-of-christian-moms-with-lgbt -children1/.

son, and that we are important to the Church. Instead my entire family is now out of the church we served in and called home for over 20 years, because of the alienation and separation.

I want them to know that I dream of being able to seek God's will together in this, admitting none of us have all the answers, acknowledging the strong emotions we all bring to the table, and realizing we may end up disagreeing. I want them to know I miss them, and I hope one day we'll be able to share our lives again.

The responses were overwhelming in their beauty and in their raw honesty about the damage the Church has done in their journey, just how much of a barrier Christians have been to them and to their children since coming out. These were wounds I'd always realized were there, but hearing them with this clarity and so concentrated was powerfully moving. Soon after that they asked me to be their honorary pastor. I was humbled by the invitation and grateful that they trusted me enough to welcome me into their stories, but at the same time it broke my heart because it reminded me just how the Church has failed them and so many like them. Most of these women have church families, or at least they had them at one time. They already had pastors in their lives who knew them and knew their children, people who should be caring for them and living alongside them—but who are not. They shared the stories of the alienation and distance they've experienced from pastors, ministers, and church friends. I call this the "second closet."

When students are both gay and Christian (and yes, you can be both), they live knowing that they have to hide everything all the time. They become experts at concealing attraction, at hiding visual cues, at steering conversations away from potentially awkward moments, especially in the Church. It isn't like they haven't been warned. They've sat through the worship services, heard all the sermons, know all the Scripture passages, and seen all the protests. Most LGBTQ teens raised in the Church know exactly what the Church thinks of them. They can't avoid it, even living in secret. They realize that in most cases, coming out is simply not an option, and so they stay hidden in the closet: alone, isolated, suffocated. And even when they do come out, they don't really get out. If these young people, in moments of exhaustion or anger or complete desperation, do share that deepest of secrets with their Christian parents, and even if those parents do choose not to disown them or expel them, something else happens almost instantly: the whole family goes into the closet together, into a second hiding.

Once they learn the truth (or have the long-feared truth verbalized to them), parents so often realize that they've inherited the stigma of their children's sexuality. It's as if they discovered that their son or daughter had some contagious illness and now they're basically quarantined along with them, corporate victims of the devastating distance that the Church has so easily and willingly created from individuals in the LGBTQ community. They find the table no longer has room for them as they are. Families in the second closet share similar patterns: they begin to skip church outings, they stop attending small group meetings, they more frequently opt out of Sunday services, not because they no longer want those things and not because they don't have a hunger for deep community and spiritual nurturing, but because they fear that they no longer belong. In many cases, they are told quite explicitly that they don't. A child's sexuality often makes the entire family feel like discarded orphans in their spiritual community. The emotional toll on those in the second closet is incalculable, especially the LGBTQ students themselves. Not only do they bear the burden of their own personal secret, but they get strapped with the additional millstone of guilt for shoving their parents and siblings into the shadows as well. This is one of the Church's greatest shared sins.

These mothers have made expanding the table their life's work because they know better than most what it's like to be excluded. Just as it was for Jesus, compassion is the thing they default to when they look at the crowds. They've also dug deeper into the bedrock of their theology than most homophobic/transphobic pastors ever will, because they've had to for their children's sake. Coming face-to-face with the bigotry of the church, they've examined the Scriptures tirelessly, and they've asked the most difficult of questions about God and love and family. In the process they've discarded bulky, cumbersome layers of dogma and tradition, and found the fiercely beating heart of Jesus beneath it all. In them and in their community together, there is a purity and depth of vulnerability that most churches never dream of having. It is messy and costly, and it is filled with grace. I am learning how to be more like Jesus by watching them love their children and one another well.

In recent months I've been introduced to the Mama Dragons, a parallel LGBTQ moms' group in the Mormon Church who were inspired by the Bears to offer similar support for those in their faith tradition. Their name came out of the realization that their road was perhaps even more treacherous and brutal than even a bear could manage. They would need to be stronger and fiercer and have a belly full of fire to meet the challenge of caring for their children in such a hostile environment. In a Church marked by perhaps even greater secrecy and more vulnerable to shunning than even the conservative evangelical denominations, many of them have had to deprogram the guilt wired into them just to begin reconciling their religion and their children's reality. They often end up fighting openly for their children while battling their own inner demons about their gender identity and sexual orientation.

During one of my first telephone conversations with one of the women who launched the group, she said to me, "The more I walk down this road, the bigger God becomes." This is almost always the by-product of expanding the table: God is right-sized. Rarely, if ever, do you do the work of hospitality, authenticity, diversity, and agenda-free relationships and encounter a smaller, more selective God. The Mama Dragons are stepping beyond the constraints of their tradition and finding a wide-open space where they can be both fully spiritual and fully authentic. It's been a wonderful blessing not only to meet these extraordinarily brave women, but also to introduce them to one another. I recently received a selfie from a Bear and a Dragon having lunch together. I was grateful for the road I've been on and the lives I've intersected as I've walked it. I'm especially thankful that I now get to sit with these women.

The bigger table connects people in ways that eclipse the sometimes jagged, bloody road we travel to get there. I was able to meet another Mama Bear at a table gathering hosted by a friend in Northern California. We exchanged hugs as if we were family who'd been reunited after decades apart (because we are exactly that). God had allowed our paths to cross as each of us were doing the work and garnering the bruises of making a more loving, inclusive Church. Later that evening, as a group of us gathered around a table filled with hors d'oeuvres and a selection of local wine, this Mama Bear said, "I found your post just before my daughter came out. I had no idea you were talking to me. But because I'd read it, when she shared her truth with me—I didn't blow it." There was something in words I had written months earlier and thousands of miles away that gave her the encouragement she needed to begin this new season with her daughter differently than she would have otherwise. If I'd never pushed to expand the table where I was, I'd have never gotten fired, and I'd never have been free to publish the post I did, and that mama's daughter might not have received as loving and encouraging a response as she had. This isn't a testament to my writing, but to what happens when we push against the bigotry and fear that can tend to keep our tables small: we find others doing the same thing. When we are faithful, God connects our dots.

Last winter I attended a conference for LGBTQ Christians and ministry allies being held in Houston. A bunch of the Bears, along with some spouses and adult children, had scheduled a dinner at the hotel, and I was fortunate enough to get an invitation. It was something to see. We filled up a huge chunk of the restaurant's massive dining room, sharing

hugs, comparing family photos, taking selfies, telling stories—
and laughing until we were out of breath. Without needing to
name it, *this* was the Church, as real and powerful as it gets. No
worship service, no preaching, no Bible study; just a table and
a group of people fully *for* one another, sharing life together,
reflecting Jesus to one another.

I recently had a conversation with the distraught mother
of nineteen-year-old Danny, who had always wanted to be a
youth minister. He'd spent countless hours after school and on
weekends volunteering at his church. He'd led worship with
the student band, was personally mentored by his youth pastor toward his chosen vocation, and was excitedly preparing to
attend seminary after college. One afternoon three years ago,
after several years of concealing it, Danny came out to his pastor. That was the last time he stepped foot in that or any other
church. Upon his revelation, Danny was instantly removed
from ministry, made a pariah in his peer community, publicly humiliated by church elders, and given an ultimatum of
conversion therapy or expulsion. I still remember his mother's
words, delivered through heavy sobs to me, a complete stranger
until just moments earlier: "My son loved Jesus. All he wanted
to do his whole life was to serve God and care for people, and
now he wants nothing to do with the Church or Christianity."
Danny's mother and her son were in that second closet, and
they were enduring it all alone. They had lost a place at the
table, and both they and the Church were suffering for it. This
can't be acceptable to us, regardless of our theology. We have
to find a way to bridge the distance in our theologies and allow
all people to have dignity and loving community.

I never knew Mama Bears and Mama Dragons existed when
I wrote the "If I Have Gay Children" post, just as I didn't
know what the Gay Christian Network was, or Level Ground
or the Restoration Project, or the millions of people of all faith
traditions who would read my words about my children and
find them resonating within them—and that's the story here
of the bigger table. You may need to speak first, so that others
who may not have the strength or the opportunity to speak

can find their voices. You and I have no idea of the goodness out there until we seek and speak our truest truth. Once we do, God lets you see things you'd never see any other way. The Church can learn a lot from the Mama Bears and Mama Dragons about hospitality and authenticity and diversity and expectation-less community. I'm praying we will listen more closely to them, and more importantly to their children, and that we will become as faithful, forgiving, and openhearted as they are. If that happens, the table will expand beyond what we imagine, and we will find ourselves sitting across from people who show us a God we didn't think we'd ever see.

16

A Pastor, a Rabbi, and an Imam Walk into a Bar

Real love is contagious. It is infectious. When something is purely of God, it can't be contained within the walls we fashion for it. This kind of love always yields a fruit that can't be managed or manufactured or scheduled. Jesus said this was the expectation-defying, unpredictable activity of the Spirit that would characterize his people (John 3:8). This was the movement of the early Church, a movement that grew exponentially in a way that modern churches all want to replicate but rarely can because we're all trying to engineer man-made miracles. We craft baptism events, we schedule worship nights, we plan revivals. We so love to talk about following the Spirit's leading, but in practice we really want to run the show and get God to work for us. One of the most freeing lessons I ever learned as a pastor is that I cannot do spiritual things; I can only do physical things. I can only respond in flesh and blood to what I believe God is saying, and then rest in the results. God is the only One who can do soul stuff. My most pressing job as a pastor is often to get out of the way—and it ain't easy.

A number of people who responded to my "If I Have Gay Children" letter shared that in the piece they somehow found permission to express what they'd been feeling, the questions they'd had, the doubts they'd been concealing. One of the revelatory aspects of having something reach an audience that large is realizing just how much unspoken, unshared, unprocessed junk we are all carrying. I started to see the sheer number of people who were all longing for something more from faith community but had no safe space to speak that longing. And while that specific post may have tapped into something in a specific way, really it wasn't as much about the words themselves as it was about their honesty. It was about the desire so many people have to be fully transparent in a community where such authenticity is treasured and practiced. That conspiracy of silence we talked about earlier is exhausting and it's heavy, and when people begin to feel the freedom to be real and open, the lightness returns. To hear a Christian and a pastor openly express love for the LGBTQ community and to push back against their accepted orthodoxy made people feel they had a kindred spirit. Maybe you're reading this book for that reason. Some people have used that post as a discussion starter in their church staff meetings, in small groups, or at kitchen tables, and that's one of the great realities of the bigger table: the way it allows us to encourage and come alongside complete strangers without even realizing it. Sometimes our simple, clear words of truth can be for others the place they stand on to begin speaking their own. When we find affinity in the heart of another, we start to feel less alien, less odd, less fearful about who we are, and it releases the voice we'd kept buried for fear that it was the only one like it. This is how goodness goes viral.

And it's not just people from a Christian background who feel compelled to break the conspiracy of silence. I've talked to people from every faith tradition and worldview wrestling with how their faith community treats the LGBTQ community. One of those people was Avi Orlov, an Orthodox rabbi from New York City. Soon after the "If I Have Gay Children" post was published, he drafted and published his own response, sharing his heart for his children from his perspective as a Jewish father and religious leader and teacher. The *Huffington Post* picked up his piece, and it too had begun to travel around the world. We connected soon after, and just as with my Mama Bear meeting, it was very much a feeling of reunited family, the sense of kinship that is so often what those building a more open religious community invariably have regardless of the tradition they come from. We spent an hour trading life stories, talking about our families, and in particular sharing our journey toward becoming fully LGBTQ-affirming clergy, and the unique challenges of doing the work in our particular religious contexts. Avi has become a dear friend, and whenever we talk we continue to marvel at the greater and far bigger thing happening in the world within people of faith. We both have seen the same beautiful movement in our very different settings, one that transcends what we grew up believing defined God's work and God's people. Avi is a rabbi of the bigger table. We're building together.

The place where God is will always be radically inclusive. It will always outgrow the container, always break beyond the borders we create or imagine or intend. The bigger table will always be leading us beyond where we believe the edge of our compassion and connection should be, and often this will be outside the rigid faith of our childhood. This is the work Jesus did in the Jewish people who comprised the core of his inner circle. His call on their lives was to move beyond Judea and Samaria, "and to the ends of the earth" (Acts 1:8). It's easy to miss the subversive nature of this directive. Can you imagine being an observant Jew raised to believe that the Gentiles were outside of the blessing of God, and then to be told that this is who you are to take the message to? How audacious, how shocking, how downright heretical it would have seemed? (Almost as counterintuitive as loving your enemies and blessing those who curse you.) Thank God that God is always going to be better at inclusion than we are; always more compassionate, more loving, more forgiving. We can't out-love God. Our selfishness prevents it. We'll always default to protection, to exclusion, to comfort, and these things will be barriers that we will always need to be aware of and push hard

against. God is always going to be interfaith, and the people
of God will be too.

Your religion might be one of those very barriers, and this
may be the most challenging part of the bigger table for you
if you've been raised in a very strict parochial tradition. It's
certainly the biggest objection that comes from many of my
Christian brothers and sisters: "If you're this open to people of
other faiths and you don't have an agenda to share the gospel,"
they often ask, "why are you still calling it a Christian community? What is left that is distinct?" The answer I give these
folks is that Jesus spent all of his life with non-Christians. This
may sound like a snarky exercise in semantics, but it's truer
than we usually realize. Jesus lived and ministered in the midst
of a world that was only beginning to know him. Every single
person he shared life with was, in a sense, outside his spiritual
tradition, because as we discussed last chapter, he was defining
that tradition with each breath and word. There was no need
to insulate himself from humanity, no religious bubble to stay
sequestered in, no threat from those whose beliefs were diver-
gent from his. He was doing a new thing. He immersed himself in that which was not like him so that they could know
him. Jesus' ministry was a fully interfaith endeavor, and that is
perhaps the place where the Christian Church has corporately
dropped the ball most spectacularly. We've wanted to claim
we love *the world* as Jesus did, while separating ourselves from
a great majority of it. We tend to live with a harsh, binary
filter. We see the Church—and then everyone else. We see
Christians—and we see all the other people. There is almost
no way to fully expand the table with this as our default operating system. Christians need a new way of being in the world
that truly embraces other theological traditions and the people
in those traditions. Throughout his life and ministry, Jesus
was always redefining who the neighbor was, the neighbor we
were called to love as ourselves. He also redefined who could
be the hero.

In Luke's Gospel, Jesus tells a parable (a kind of spiritually
loaded word picture)—which, even if you're not a particularly

religious person, you're probably vaguely familiar with—commonly known as the parable of the Good Samaritan (10:30–37). Synopsis: *A lone traveler is attacked by bandits and left bloodied and penniless by the side of the road. Two religious folks (a priest and a Levite) passing by both ignore the wounded man, but a Samaritan stops, binds up his wounds, gets a room for him, and pays for the man's care during his recovery.*

To those not familiar with the scene and the characters Jesus uses or with his audience, the moral of the story might seem like just another feel-good message, "Be kind to others in need," but it's far more scandalous and subversive than that. Jesus, a first-century Jew, was speaking to other first-century Jews who treasured the purity of their bloodline and despised the racially blended Samaritans whom they believed to be contaminated. That Jesus, a rabbi, would make the Samaritan the hero of the story at all (especially when favorably compared to Jewish characters) was a brutal sucker punch to the gut of his listeners and a brazen warning not to overestimate one's own righteousness and another's moral inferiority. It was a specific elevating of the *despised other*.

Most of us like to identify our Samaritans and to get them in the crosshairs of our righteous outrage. We still bend more toward choosing sides and defining our enemies and labeling evil and identifying villains than we do toward understanding people. It strikes me that we who comprise the Church are still missing the clear truth that God is fully alive in every person we encounter; that every "Samaritan" is potentially our teacher. I'm more aware of this truth than ever before as I watch my fellow believers interact with people, especially in America following the election. As Christians confident in our own moral position, we so easily adopt a posture of self-righteousness that rarely takes time to consider the damage *we* may be doing out there, the suffering *we* might be conveniently walking past, the inherent arrogance embedded in *our* religious convictions. We so often assume that the enemy of humanity must be across the aisle or across town or in another country. We almost never court the possibility that it could be in the mirror.

Jesus wasn't pulling any punches here in the Samaritan's story, and that's important to remember. His intended audience would have been rightly pissed off. He was not merely a placid, gentle teddy bear who only dispensed sweet words and candy kisses. Sometimes Jesus was a savage lion who ripped religious folks to shreds to expose their hardened hearts and publicly call them to the carpet, challenging them to dig deeper in their expression of faith. Whether in a tax collector turned disciple, a Roman centurion professing faith, a Samaritan role model, Jesus repeatedly tells those who would listen that God is so much bigger than their expectations. He is still saying that. I wonder if we who claim Christ can still handle his difficult words. I wonder if we are still willing to listen to him when we don't get to be the hero or when he tells us we are being the uncaring bystander turning away from suffering. I wonder if we stick with the story when Jesus flips the script.

I met Jason Bennett a couple of years ago. Jason is a Christian and the director of the Murfreesboro Cold Patrol, a homeless outreach and advocacy group in the Nashville area. In October 2015, Jason saw the escalation of anti-Muslim rhetoric in his community, and as the news broke of numerous protests at mosques nationwide, he felt burdened to respond in a way that emulated Jesus, in a way he didn't see the Church responding. He reached out to Abdou Kattih, the director of the Murfreesboro Muslim Youth, a community nonprofit that promotes and organizes community service among the Muslim youth in Murfreesboro, Tennessee. They and other local faith leaders talked about how they could make a nonviolent statement together in opposition to the impending protest of the building of a mosque there.

Abdou suggested that they have a picnic and invite the whole community, in order to promote an atmosphere of peace and understanding, and to begin to organize shared community service together. He suggested that they call it Love Your Neighbor, in the spirit of the second greatest commandment issued by Jesus. The multifaith, multigenerational response was so overwhelming that they moved to do three such gatherings a year. Now coming up on their one-year anniversary, Love Your Neighbor had the most successful picnic to date, with four hundred people of all traditions and religious worldviews breaking bread and sharing stories. Their gatherings have organically created many additional opportunities for people to come together aside from the picnics. Every month the Murfreesboro Muslim Youth holds interfaith social outings for teenagers. They've also started an initiative for youth called Face 2 Face, an activity designed to promote friendships and understanding between youth of diverse backgrounds.

Most recently, Love Your Neighbor has collaborated with the Faith and Culture Center of Nashville to bring a program called A Seat at the Table to Murfreesboro. It's an adult program set around a dinner table, allowing people to get to know others from diverse backgrounds. Jason says of those involved in this growing ministry, "Our lives are so much richer as we've intentionally sought to know one another." Jason's personal burden, and his ability to see compassion and not contempt when looking at the humanity in front of him, set something in motion that is far beyond what his dream was. That simple act of one person moving has allowed hundreds and hundreds of people's paths to cross that would never have any other way: not through church services, outreach events, or street preaching—and certainly not through sermons shouted from a distance, theological wall building, or mosque protests. Due in great part to people like Jason and Abdou reaching to one another beyond their faith traditions, the mosque was built.

This is what happens when the table expands, friends. This is why this matters to all of us, because it teaches all of us. It fills in the gaps we didn't know we had in our image of God. We find ourselves pulled into the lives of people we'd never otherwise meet, and they show divinity in ways we've never encountered it and couldn't in any other way. When we move toward others with compassion, we get a front-row seat to the work of God, and this is one of the priceless gifts that I've been working to give people still in the cloistered religious bubble, still seeing the other as threat, still satisfied with a small table. Contrary to some teaching in the Church, this kind of intentional cross-pollination of faith traditions isn't a dilution of any of them—it's a reaffirmation of the best things of each of them. There isn't competition. These traditions don't have to serve as hills we claim and defend. They are simply the beautiful thing that compels us to love the other well. Part of agenda-free relationship is trusting the spiritual experiences of others, especially when they don't match our own. That's a huge challenge in organized Christianity, which seeks ownership of the Divine.

I grew up in the Church believing that my faith made me superior; that I was somehow further ahead, more enlightened, closer to God than everyone else. I was taught that my job description as a card-carrying follower of Jesus came with the expectation that I would engage with people outside of my spiritual community with the hope of eventually correcting them, fixing them, and saving them. There's an insidious condescension inherent in this religious worldview, one that doesn't really take any cues from Jesus, and it's one the people of the bigger table are looking to let go of.

This is the rub, for we who say we believe that each person bears the image of God. If this is *really* true for us, we will not hesitate to be a student of their lives and to be unapologetic in seeing a facet of who God is in them—and even in the expression of their religion. Whatever is real and true about God will be revealed in our midst, and it will testify to itself. We won't need to claim it, own it, or commandeer it. We'll just be present and be reverent in the face of it. The question becomes whether or not you can unlearn enough to be OK with this. How much stretching are you comfortable with? If it isn't the kind of stretching that Jesus' disciples had to do, then you're probably not yet building what Jesus was building.

17
Fear Less

One of the great comforts in my travels to build a bigger table and to right-size God has been a simple reality that I've embraced, one that I hope seeps deep into your heart whatever your theological leanings are: *God is not out to squash you.* This is an incredibly difficult truth to claim if you've experienced religion through the lens of fear that told you otherwise.

I grew up believing that God loved me dearly. I also grew up believing God was very angry with me. I was taught that God personally created me and yet was immediately displeased by my sinfulness. So my very earliest identity was forged in the crucible of this unsettling duplicity: I was both adored and resented by my Creator. As a child I lived in the tension of being the object of both the wrath and the love of God simultaneously. As I grew, I was told I needed to find and do and believe what would tip the scales from punishment to reward, from damnation to salvation, from abandonment to blessing. I had to remove the massive barrier between myself and God, to bridge the wide expanse between the two of us—which somehow was *me*. For simply *being*, the problem was me. Apologize for my inborn transgressions and I earned the right to be

God's child. One wrong move, one doctrinal deviation, one errant belief, though, and I would be toast. Living always in paradox, I learned that I had a tender, caring Maker who knit me together in my mother's womb, numbered every hair on my head—and was never far from destroying me for the birth defect I'd inherited somewhere in the process.

Through adolescence and adulthood I stumbled and strained, trying to win the affections and approval of a Creator who'd given me life without my consent and then required me to spend that life figuring out how to earn forgiveness from something I'd never done—other than take my first breath. And I was to be grateful. I was taught to have joy in my rescue, to find good news in being pardoned, to celebrate dodging a bullet. I was told to sing songs of praise to God for rescuing me from what this same God had wanted to do to me in the first place. I was to celebrate that Jesus was the gift and sign that God didn't really want to punish me, that his blood was a substitute for my own. I was first pronounced guilty before God, and then made to feel guilty for the cross: responsible for Christ's death because of my filthy mess. And into this terrifying journey came the endless parade of gatekeepers and finger pointers: the ones so willing to assess my performance from a distance, to point out my failures, to correct my conclusions, to critique my behavior, to determine my destination. They gladly placed themselves between me and God, magnifying the distance, adding to the obstacles, amplifying the guilt, compounding the difficulty. Guilt is a hell of a drug to try and come off of. The detox can be brutal. I know because even though I'm three years into my recovery from being a Christian know-it-all, I still have the occasional tremors that come when the muscle memory of my childhood faith kicks in and I begin to wonder if God is angry with me for any number of things I may be getting wrong. Many times I feel certain of it and it paralyzes me, at least temporarily. I see vivid pictures of the eternal suffering I'm surely earning by rejecting God, until I recognize that this is the voice of the people of the small table echoing in my head: the self-righteous stone throwers, eager to dispense judgment from a distance.

This is true of many of us on this road of reexamining everything. When your table expands and you're forced to challenge the religious system you grew up in, sometimes the box you placed God in simply can't accommodate the change, and you need a new one. Some call this faith deconstruction or the great unraveling—but practically speaking, it usually feels like free-falling into the abyss—or it all hitting the fan. When you find yourself no longer at home in the religion of your past, the existential crisis can be devastating. You grieve the loss of something you were once so certain of, and with the bottom dropping out you wonder if you'll be left with anything reliable to hold on to or stand upon. It's all quite terrifying, and I want you to know that I understand.

Leveraging this fear is all too often the bread and butter of the traditional Church. When we question doctrine, when we push back against tradition, when we express dissatisfaction with the current system, we often find religious people around us are all too happy to heap regret and guilt upon our shoulders and to dole out damnation. We can go from loved one to leper in an instant, and quickly end up on the outside of our own spiritual community looking in from a distance we can't bridge. You may have experienced similar alienation as you've started this journey. This guilt may be familiar right now. In these times it's important to remember your road, to remind yourself of the path that led you here; to remember that this was not some premeditated, willful decision to discard your previous faith convictions, but simply the unavoidable evolution *of* those convictions. This is part of the same journey that once led you to orthodoxy, the same God who has walked with you. It's important to hold on to the truth that honest doubts and unresolved questions acquired in authentic pursuit of God are far more productive than maintaining a flashy veneer of unshakable faith.

These questions *can* be worked through organically in the context of the bigger table. When we are living in a spiritual community where radical hospitality, total authenticity, true diversity, and agenda-free relationships are the normal operating system, every question is not only manageable but welcome, because our default condition becomes hope and not fear. We don't come burdened with shame, we don't come fearful of expulsion, and we don't spend our time waiting for the judgmental shoe to drop. When people come to the bigger table, they don't need to earn acceptance—this is a given. When we gather at the table Jesus sets, none of us are misfits. By our very presence we fit, because we are full image bearers of God and beloved as we are, without alteration. The traditional Church tends to favor a clearly defined, very narrow *inside* and *outside*, and this is where many people part ways because they find their messy, gritty reality doesn't feel compatible with such clear delineation. But when everyone is openly bringing everything, there's real connection—when each person realizes they are not outsiders around the table.

For much of my life, this guilt, pressure, and fear of exposure had left me fairly exhausted. But I am slowly but surely walking into a new story, gradually but most definitely jettisoning those things that don't ring true anymore and traveling much lighter. My reverence for God has never been greater, my wonder never more full, my desire to know my Maker never stronger. The difference is, I now see God through the lens of one who is beloved, not one who is beloved with conditions. Life now is not a test to try and *reach* God, but an opportunity to notice God. I am seeking Jesus more deeply than ever—not to escape punishment, but to discover life as it is best lived. My faith is not about fleeing something horrible, but running toward something beautiful. I am daily responding in gratitude for the beauty of the gift of this world, not in the hope I can eventually escape it. I come to the Scriptures now not as divine dictation, but as the journal entries of those who came before me and who have walked this road of asking, seeking, and knocking. They are not a road map, but a traveling companion. And in all that I do not know, I am walking in the safety and security of trusting that

I never was the enemy of God, that I am made of whatever God is made of.

A few years ago, I lost the desire to pray. I lost the ability to pray. For a Christian and a pastor, this is more than mildly disconcerting. My swirling doubt and the things I was seeing and thinking began to leave me dry and ambivalent about talking with God. But I knew the Scriptures, I knew the platitudes, and I knew that I was to pray unceasingly (and in fact was told by a well-meaning friend that I should "pray about it"). So one evening I endeavored again to pray through my reticence to prayer, and a few seconds into the exercise, I interrupted myself. "God," I spoke within my head, "you *know* I don't want to pray right now, and you know every reason *why* I don't want to pray. You know all the stuff that I'm feeling, and you know every frustration. You better than anyone else know what's happening within me, so I'm not going to fake this. I'm not going to pray, and I trust that you understand that this is the most authentic prayer I have right now." I return again and again to this place, to the belief that God is fully aware of the road you and I are on, that God is far more merciful and forgiving than we would ever be with one another or with ourselves. My prayers are different now because of it.

After all, this is God we're talking about. If God is everything we've been led to believe God is, God has such patience with us that, were we to embrace it, it would make us rightly fearless. And once the fear of "getting it wrong" departs we can be completely ourselves, sharing the full contents of our hearts—hopefully with God's people, but at the very least with God.

Hell is a pretty terrible thing to build a faith on anyway. Living each difficult day here in a fire-and-brimstone spirituality rooted in your own moral filth is a fairly tragic way to spend your few short decades on the planet, yet that's what far too many Christians do and have been doing for hundreds of years. And if they haven't necessarily intentionally constructed such a religion based in fear and punishment avoidance, they've certainly inherited one and have grown up from birth firmly planted in the belief that God is out to squash them—because he loves them. This is the paradoxical heart of the bulk of our traditional Christian orthodoxy: God so loves us that he sent Christ to die in our place, saving us from the correct penalty of death for our sin (a penalty, by the way, that he alone demands). Yet this gracious reprieve from eternal punishment only comes with us acknowledging both our depravity in utero and our need to be exonerated from a guilt we acquired simply by being born. The whole thing runs primarily not on love, but on damnation—at least in the hands of the preachers and the Pharisees and those who peddle the heavy fear that millions of people of the faith become hopelessly saddled with:

> Fear of believing the wrong thing
>
> Fear of not praying enough
>
> Fear of joining the wrong denomination
>
> Fear of not exegeting Scripture correctly
>
> Fear of not evangelizing our neighbors enough
>
> Fear of Muslims and gays and atheists
>
> Fear of beer and Harry Potter and cuss words and yoga and mandalas and voting Democrat
>
> Fear of a God who is holding hell over our heads—
>
> Fear as our default setting

I lived this story for years. I preached it. I fully bought into this narrative of an angry God needing to be placated. I understand the reason it works and the crushing effect it has on us when we embrace it, and I know how disorienting it is to be compelled to cling to a loving Creator while simultaneously being taught to be terrified of what that Creator wants to do to you if you don't cling correctly. It hasn't happened in an instant, and I can't quite say how I got here, but I am simply living in a different story now. I still have God and Jesus and the Holy Spirit—but I don't have fear anymore the way I used to. That isn't to say that I don't have "the fear of the Lord" that the Bible speaks of, that awe and wonder that recognizes my smallness and God's indescribable scale and beauty. In fact, my view of God is as expansive and reverent and breathtaking as it's ever been. It just isn't defined by the rigid Christian narrative of my childhood that says I am an enemy of God at birth.

If God is God, then God is intimately aware of the path you're on. God sees your striving, your desire to know, your efforts to love better, and so even when these things take you from tradition or orthodoxy or surety, there can be peace there and trust that God is present. Looking at the long, meandering road you've been on, how can you possibly define some precise pass-fail in all of that? If you feel the table of your hospitality expanding, if you feel the container you had for God being shattered, if you yourself are being drawn to something deeper than the religion of your past, that is the pull of God. It is the extravagant, barrier-breaking, tradition-transcending heart of Jesus that is demanding to be yielded to. To the gatekeepers and the finger pointers, this surrender to God will look like rebellion. They will demand guilt for the conclusions you've come to and repentance from the path you're on. You will need to be steadfast and rest in the love that casts out all fear. They will snicker and condemn and dismiss. They will name this heresy. They will call this a mutiny. To you, it is a progression.

In Matthew's Gospel, Jesus warned that following him would generate turbulence for us, that it might create fault lines in our closest relationships (Matt. 10:16–22). We always assume that the divide he spoke of would be between ourselves and those around us who are not Christians. Again, this is the starkly drawn, dualistic, inside-outside way we've come to view faith. But seeking to reflect Jesus more fully often places us in direct conflict with those who share our faith tradition, and even with that very tradition itself. This is why the Pharisees so resisted Christ: because their old-wineskin hearts could not accommodate the fresh outpouring of the Spirit. Obedience to the new thing God is doing in us may bring friction and condemnation. It may challenge those we live with, worship next to, and minister alongside. This may be the very holy ground Jesus calls us to because it is the place we more fully bring the kingdom. Refuse to feel guilt for this road. You know how you got here and you know Who is with you—and *for* you. Fear not.

18

Is the Table Really Big Enough?

Being an optimist is hazardous duty these days.

Right now I'm nearly two years into the daily work of building faith communities that embody radical hospitality, true diversity, real authenticity, and agenda-free community. In many ways I feel like I'm the same person I was when I started forty years ago. I still feel like the same little boy with the same big God: still filled with wonder, still overflowing with hope, still certain that our best days are ahead of us. Often I'm moved to tears and covered in goose bumps as I meet people on this same path of expanding the table. I see them shedding old prejudices, reaching across former divides, and seeking new ways of expressing the audacious love of an eternal God. They remind me of just how much goodness is still here in this place, and they point toward what can and should be. They are so often the very thing that fuels me to keep going. They help me hold on to the eyes of compassion, which isn't easy.

I've been a pastor in the local church for the better part of two decades, and I've seen a lot more than I probably wanted to when I was that little boy. For most of that time, I've believed that the table was big enough for everyone, that the

Church could be a place where disparate souls could gather together and find enough commonality to transcend their differences. I always thought that real diversity, even theological diversity in the Church, wasn't only aspirational but also possible. I've always believed that when Jesus was truly present in the hearts of people, this would be enough to bridge the other divides within them, divides of race and gender and sexuality and politics. I still believe that, but it is a daunting task at times. As I look at the Christian church that *is*, I see so much that needs mending.

The far extremes of the Right and the Left have grown frighteningly similar; each expends great energy vilifying the other. The former broker in fear of the other's perceived immorality, the latter in anger at the other's apparent intolerance. Those with privilege so often resist change, desperate to keep power that does not belong to them. Those who've been marginalized clamor for justice but rarely seem able to celebrate those days it makes a welcome appearance. Each side spends little time listening or seeking compromise, and much of the time identifying deal breakers, looking for justification to shut down conversation, walk away, and write the other off. The loud, angry fringes of our faith have become so conditioned to the fight that they've nearly lost the ability to communicate unless it is with war rhetoric and battle postures. They forgo real, messy, costly relationship in favor of lazy shouts from a distance, too easily sacrificing any compassion on the altar of their activism. I see a whole lot of venom and very little grace, a great deal of name-calling and not much forgiveness, a boatload of condemnation and not many mea culpas.

More and more, the work of expanding the table is moving me to try and find a solid place in the middle and to pull these opposing factions toward one another to commonality, to affinity, to humanity. That's the very heart of this beautiful expansion we're all longing for, which is probably the greatest challenge you and I face in this desire for redemptive spiritual community. It places us in the middle of unfathomable tension. It puts us on the very front lines of bigotry and fear and earns us the scars and bruises that come when trying to engineer a truce in the middle of a war zone. This is where our call to Christlikeness is most urgent, where it is most needed.

In the eyes of so many people in the world, Christians no longer have much in common with Jesus, and often we've fully earned this. We have become all-or-nothing religious extremists who take Jesus' name in vain by using him only to further our cause, win our arguments, or justify our positions. They believe that most of us have little interest in allowing him to alter our hearts when it comes to making peace with those we consider our adversaries, that we don't really want to *emulate* Jesus as much as we want to name-drop him in arguments. We want him to sanction our words and our responses and our politics, even when they bear little resemblance to him. We want carte blanche to be as mean-spirited and rude and arrogant and unforgiving as we like—and to still call it faithfulness. We seek to deem ourselves rightly religious with little to no alteration in our agendas and preferences. We demand that others love us as we desire to be loved, and we really don't give much of a damn about what we're supposed to be offering *them,* whether they love us or not. This is the proving ground for the people of the bigger table. This is where we see what we're made of and who we want to become.

I was heading to Portland, Oregon, for an LGBTQ Christian conference just after my "If I Have Gay Children" post went viral. Patty, one of my readers there, messaged me and asked if I'd be interested in hosting a meet-up at a restaurant for other area followers of the blog. I told her I thought it was a great idea (though I secretly imagined it would just be Patty, my wife, and me). In her optimism, Patty reserved a large table at a local burger spot, and on that Saturday we arrived early to welcome anyone who might show up. And one by one the table began filling up. With each arrival there were warm embraces with strangers, like lifelong friends being reunited. The next couple of hours flew by, as we shared stories, talked life and faith, and *broke bread* (filled with copious amounts of meat and cheese). It was about as sweet a time and as special a meal as I'd been a part of, and I didn't want to see it end. I don't think any of us did. It felt like home.

We were a wildly diverse assortment of humanity gathered around that table, across lines of gender, theology, and orientation, but because we'd all been introduced through the threshold of the blog, every person knew they were already welcome. They came to that table knowing they had nothing to prove, no theological boxes to check or religious hoops to jump through. We had decidedly different roads and spiritual convictions, but we all came knowing that this wouldn't be a hindrance. It felt free and real—and holy.

My wife and I talked on the trolley home about the meal. We'd both realized that this was what we wanted to be part of. This was what was possible. I still speak to most of my tablemates from that day, and they remain special to me because they made something real to me: a broader, wider, more authentic expression of intentional community that welcomed the mess. They are a huge part of the writing of this book and the work I do.

I really want God to be big enough. I want the table to be big enough. I still seek a Church that is not the least but the most diverse place on the planet. I still dream that the life of Christ can be fully incarnated in the people who bear his name. I want this faith to produce something more redemptive than choosing sides and building silos and pointing fingers. I want it to generate hope and yield goodness and produce mercy in ways that defy description and explanation and denying. I am holding out hope for true communion. But it's really not up to me alone. It's in the hands of *you* who claim faith in Jesus, from wherever you find yourself standing and however you align yourself and whatever you see your personal calling as a Christian to be. And it's up to you, regardless of your faith tradition or religious affiliation. It's about the eyes with which you choose to see this life, this world, yourself, and the other.

I wonder if *you* believe the table really is big enough for you, for those you love, for those you find difficult to love, for those who have little love for you. Because ultimately if you do, you have a decision to make: You're either going to be a builder—or you're not. You're either going to deny yourself and take up the costly cross of sacrifice and keep seeking to come humbly, or you're going to defiantly barricade yourself within your rightness and your righteousness and wait for the check to come. You're either going to try to live as a selfless servant or look to die a spiteful martyr. I still do believe in the bigger table, but it's more difficult than ever to keep that faith, probably because the resistance to it is so great. We have to be the resistance to that resistance. In the face of a loud hatred, we need to be a louder, more loving response. We have to become activists of goodness.

I'm hoping this page won't be the end for you. I'm hoping it will begin another chapter in your story. I'm hoping this is a launching pad and not a landing pad. I want to encourage you to keep looking at the crowds with those eyes of compassion, through the lens of love and not fear. Show up in the middle of the noise and the mess out there and bring something redemptive. Ask anything and say everything, because you can. The only way the table around us is ever truly going to be big enough is if we all make more room within us. God has always worked this way. The kingdom has always started within. Love has always been an inside job.

Grab some wood and some tools, friend. We have work to do.

Acknowledgments

The writing of this book began nearly three years ago, but the story is much bigger than that, and that story has been filled with beautiful, loving, passionate people, many of whom are reflected in these pages, either mentioned explicitly or embedded in its fibers. Here are some of them:

To my wife, Jen, and my kids, Noah and Selah, for being the greatest partners in this life anyone could be fortunate enough to have. Your love sustains me.

To my Mom and Dad; my brothers, Brian and Eric; and my sister, Michelle, for loving me so well since even before I was born.

To all the church communities I have served, each one of them teaching and challenging me in profound, life-altering ways.

To Pastor Susan May, who called me back and invited me in.

To Doug Hammack, for helping me prepare to get fired, and to my North Raleigh Community Church family, for helping do the hard work of expanding the table in Raleigh and in my life.

To my amazing agent, Sharon Pelletier at Dystel & Goderich, for being a wonderful advocate and companion on this meandering journey.

To David Dobson, Jessica Miller Kelley, and the Westminster John Knox family, for believing that the bigger table is worth pursuing. I am grateful.

To Steve Knight, Mark Sandlin, Justin Lee, and Matthew Paul Turner, who helped me find a path out of a dark place.

To the readers of my blog *Stuff That Needs to Be Said*, for being a beautiful extended family, and for being the daily inspiration for *A Bigger Table*.

To the Mama Bears and Mama Dragons, for showing me what fierce, relentless love looks like.

To Pastor Stan Mitchell, Pastor Melissa Greene, and the entire GracePointe community for showing me what the bigger table can be. You all amaze me.

To the students and leaders of BIGHOUSE Youth in Charlotte, for being my beloved family for eight years and for inspiring me still.

To those gathered at the table in Portland, for giving me the dream of a bigger table.

To Jason Bennett, for sharing your story with me. You are an inspiration.

To my Patreon supporters, for your partnership financially, emotionally, and spiritually. You have been invaluable in my life.

To Joe, Danny, and the University of the Arts café, for helping rewrite my story of the LGBTQ community.

To everyone who has ever read, commented on, or shared my words. It is something I never take for granted.

To all those who believe that the table has to be bigger.

A Word for Pastors

Pastor, be brave.

If there's one thing I regret the most about my first two decades as a pastor, I wish I'd been braver. I wish I'd been louder, sooner. I wish I'd been more vulnerable. I wish I hadn't needed to be fired in order to have the courage to ask anything and to say everything. (All right, so that's a bunch of regrets, actually.) When I was fully entrenched in the traditional church world as a pastoral leader, I believed that my inner turmoil was an anomaly: that everything happening in me wasn't happening in those I served, ministered with, and lived alongside—and this cultivated silence in me. For so much of that time I was waiting for someone there to tell me that it was OK to not be OK—and all the while they were waiting for me to tell them. The people in my community were looking to me as a pastor to set the tone for what was acceptable, to sanction their holy discontent.

As a church leader, you drive culture change. As much as we need a decentralized Church that doesn't put all the power into one person or into only a few people, the lion's share of our faith communities still place a great emphasis on those in leadership. For better or worse, in a very tangible way, faith communities tend to take on the personality of the clergy and pastoral staff. As the leaders go, so goes the entire thing. This is why expanding the table often needs to begin with those who preach, speak, cast vision, hire, train, set calendars, and appropriate financial and human resources. You will need to be the one who breaks the conspiracy of silence by giving voice to your own inner wrestling, and by doing so, make your community a safe place to reveal doubts and to actually change their minds.

Spiritual growth is often misdiagnosed as simple vacilla-tion, or worse, "backsliding." When Christians, especially pas-tors, begin to evolve in their understanding of the Bible, their view of God, or even their core theological principles, those around them tend to hit the panic button. Often there is an overreaction around these leaders, an implication that they are somehow less faithful or less committed, when in reality the opposite is almost always true. In their desire to know God more deeply, to follow Jesus more closely, or to understand the Scriptures more completely, many pastors and church leaders find they are at odds with the status quo, which ironi-cally they often helped establish. They can find themselves in the uncomfortable position of publicly arguing with their for-mer selves. But there is plenty of precedent. In fact, we see in the apostle Paul just how the Spirit of God moves us from the trajectory we were once on, even if that trajectory was formed in pursuit of God.

The Paul we meet in the letters he writes to young church communities throughout the Roman Empire is a very differ-ent Paul from the one we first encounter in the book of Acts. There he is openly persecuting Christians, complicit in their arrest, imprisonment, and death, and doing so as a devout and learned Jew—a person of deep faith in God. After an encoun-ter with Jesus, the path of Paul's life is beautifully altered, and he finds himself defending the very faith he had assaulted. His conversion represents a 180-degree turn from where he'd been, but this change didn't represent inconsistency, heresy, hypocrisy, or worldliness. It was an honest response to the fresh revelation of God he'd received. Had Paul succumbed to the pressure to be silent for fear of being perceived as less godly, we'd be telling a far different faith story right now. And yet we in our faith communities have little tolerance for pas-tors and leaders who admit to being in a state of spiritual flux. We don't allow them to waver and never really allow them to grow either. We suppress the work of God in them. The Paul of Acts would have branded the Paul of Romans a rebellion against the Lord.

This is so often the story of leaders who expand the table. They find themselves shedding the skin of their former pastoral selves and becoming something that appears so very different from who they'd been, when in reality it was simply a natural metamorphosis. This was my story. As I moved down the road I encountered Jesus, and he caused me to disagree with the *me* I'd been. For a while I had a hard time with this, but I've learned to have grace for myself. I'm hoping the pastor I am in ten years will have similar gentleness for the one writing these pages.

My friend Stan Mitchell is the lead pastor at GracePointe Church in Franklin, Tennessee. A couple of years ago, after a long period of slow but deliberate internal movement, he and his staff made the incredibly difficult decision to publicly move toward full LGBTQ inclusion and to explicitly identify as a progressive Christian community. In a church that was already thriving, this was a bold move, one fraught with the potential for disaster. The initial tremors were massive, as they lost a good portion of their regular members and entered into a season of great upheaval. This is what the table expanding does. I visited GracePointe on a Sunday morning just as they were coming through the most tumultuous weeks of their transition. Many of the wounds were still raw. There was a tangible sense of fatigue but a fierce hope pushing up through it, a feeling that everyone was ready to move forward. Stan and I were talking just before their morning service about the risk he'd taken, the pushback he'd received, and the uncertainty still lingering. He said, "We have to make this work in the local church. We have to. We can talk all we want about diversity, but if we can't make it work in a community, it's not going to matter." The resolve, faith, and courage of Pastor Stan, Pastor Melissa Greene, and the rest of his staff were palpable—and contagious too.

The community was much smaller than it had been a few months earlier, but their table was far bigger. Those still there were only just beginning to see what they were going to look like as a local expression of the love of God. There was a defiant joy in that space that has propelled them forward. GracePointe has become home for so many who might never have found themselves in church, and it has become a brilliant beacon for Christians of a bigger table all over the country. And it all began with leaders who were brave, who spoke their truest truth to their people and invited them to do the same.

This is a difficult road, pastors. Believe me, I know it isn't easy.

Every day, you have to walk that extremely fine line between hearing and obeying the voice of God—and not ticking off the wrong people in your midst. And as bold and strong willed and successful as you may be, you have to calculate the risk and reward of what you write and preach publicly. You see which way the wind is blowing and try not to fly in the face of it too much for too long. Every pastor (even the most subversive, passionate, and outspoken one) learns to read the room. When I was working in megachurches, I knew well that I could only safely take my congregations to a certain point on issues or topics or theological perspectives. I knew pretty well where the dividing line between bold prophet and unemployed prophet was, and I danced right up to the edge of it but not beyond it if I could help it.

And believe me, most of it isn't sinister, or at least not intentionally so; it's just that self-preservation, career longevity, family security, and making sure your kids have shoes are powerful realities for all of us. Yes, ministry is a calling, but it's one that's embraced and worked out in the very real business of the Church. Anyone who tells you that tension doesn't affect them is breaking a commandment. That's why the greatest gift I ever received as a pastor was getting fired. It was like a reset button for my sense of purpose. That very day and every day since then, I've experienced the absolute joy and redemptive power of speaking complete truth: not a version of truth that could keep public perception of me in a local congregation tipped toward the favorable, not a version of truth that wouldn't upset the biggest financial givers in the church, not a version of truth that wouldn't be awkward for my senior pastor, but the full, flawed, beautiful contents of my heart as a devoted follower of

Jesus, shared in real time. I now get to openly wrestle with my doubt, to fully question why we do what we do as the Church, and to be completely honest with what I feel Jesus calling me to say and do in the world, regardless of who has a problem with it or what the repercussions might be. This isn't about a lack of accountability with regard to personal conduct or morality, but about pastors having the freedom to disclose all that is revealed to them as they seek and study and serve.

I eventually found a faith community and a group of financial sponsors who support me not so that I will give a particular opinion or regurgitate a certain doctrine, but because they affirm me and the journey I am on to hear and faithfully reflect Jesus. Their support is a gift that I can't ever really express. If you are reading this afterword and are not a pastor yourself, I hope you will encourage the pastors and ministers and church staff in your life. Encourage them to be who they are compelled and ordained by God to be, not who you desire them to be. Give them permission to be fully transparent, even if that places them in opposition to you in some fundamental way.

Pastor, I want to encourage you to speak with courage. I want to remind you of what you don't owe people. You don't owe them orthodoxy or dogma or tradition or any party line. You don't owe them a conservative or progressive stance on the issues of the day. You don't owe them predictability or a theology that makes them comfortable. If you owe the people who look to you for leadership anything, it's honesty as you lead. You owe them the most open, vulnerable, bold expression of the personal revelations you hear from God in the quiet of your own heart, regardless of the cost. Don't be overtaken by the insults of your critics or intoxicated by the applause of your allies. Never let the voices around you (as well-intentioned, sincere, and loving as they may be) ever drown out the voice of Jesus. Never let security or position or obligation prevent you from being the most authentic version of yourself that you can muster.

These are heady, vitally important times. Now more than ever, people need a Christianity that is not prepackaged, market tested, or franchise ready. They need something raw and real and dangerous, even to the Church institution itself; something that dares to veer from the safe and secure in order to be covered in the dust of Jesus. Pray, wait, listen, and when you do feel like you hear God speak to you—then say everything. This is not at all the easy road, but it is the only one that you are truly called to walk. Sunday is coming. God is speaking. People are waiting on you. Pastor, be brave.

Discussion Guide

The journey to a bigger table is one practiced in community. Consider reading and discussing this book with your small group, Sunday school class, leadership team, or simply a group of friends. Three questions for each chapter are offered below. Feel free to raise other questions as you share your thoughts on the chapters read.

Choose a reading schedule based on the number of sessions you wish to allot to the discussion:

> *Four sessions:* Intro–chapter 5; chapters 6–10; chapters 11–14; chapters 15–18
>
> *Six sessions:* Intro–chapter 2; chapters 3–5; chapters 6–7; chapters 8–10; chapters 11–14; chapters 15–18
>
> *Eight sessions:* Intro–chapter 2; chapters 3–5; chapters 6–7; chapters 8–10; chapters 11–12; chapters 13–14; chapters 15–16; chapters 17–18

INTRODUCTION: A WEDNESDAY MORNING IN NOVEMBER

1. What was your experience of and reaction to the results of the 2016 U.S. presidential election?

2. How would you describe the divisions between Americans leading up to and following the 2016 presidential election? What about the divisions between American Christians?

3. How do you envision "the bigger table"? The table may expand and contract over time—what shifts have you seen in recent weeks or months?

CHAPTER 1: FINDING MY PLACE

1. What were your faith and family life like when you were a child? How big was the metaphorical table in your faith tradition? In your family? In your own mind?

2. What experiences in your youth and young adulthood were transformative to your faith and outlook on the world?

3. When is the first time you recall meeting someone very different from you in some way? What was that experience like? How did it change you?

CHAPTER 2: WHEN IN ROME

1. Have you experienced the "coming out" of a family member or close friend—or yourself? Did the freedom of being authentic outweigh the conflict or negative reactions that resulted, or not?

2. What impact did this revelation have on your faith or that of those around you?

3. Do you think people feel safe to reveal their true selves to you? Do you know certain people who model the kind of acceptance and openness that make others feel safe? Describe those people.

CHAPTER 3: GOING AGAINST THE FAMILY

1. What have been your best and worst experiences with church?

2. When have you kept quiet with other Christians to avoid bucking the norm in some way? Do you ever contribute to creating an environment where others might feel the need to keep quiet?

3. How diverse is your church theologically and politically? How diverse do you think it can or should be?

CHAPTER 4: EARTHQUAKES AND AFTERSHOCKS

1. Has your faith ever seemed to fall apart or be gradually deconstructed? Was there a particular issue or question that led you to start reexamining your faith?

2. Did you share this journey with others? If so, did you feel shamed or supported?

3. The author says on page 44, "Doubt isn't the sign of a dead faith, not necessarily even of a sickly one. It's often the sign of a faith that is allowing itself to be tested, one that is brave enough to see if it can hold up under tension." Do you agree? What are the pros and cons of boldly questioning your faith?

CHAPTER 5: THE TRUTH SHALL GET YOU FIRED

1. Have you ever experienced outright rejection because of changes that were happening in your faith or beliefs?

2. What do you see as the barriers to the bigger table? Why is a bigger table threatening to some people? What about the bigger table feels frightening or threatening to you?

3. What gives you a feeling of freedom or lightness in your faith?

CHAPTER 6: JESUS THE TABLE SETTER

1. What is striking to you about Jesus' fellowship habits?

2. When was the last time you had a sincere, face-to-face conversation about a sensitive topic with someone who believes very differently than you do about that topic?

3. What would it look like to set a table as Jesus did? Who would you invite? How would you guide the conversation or handle conflicts that arose?

CHAPTER 7: RADICAL HOSPITALITY

1. What is wrong with "tolerance"? How does it get confused with "acceptance" or "inclusion"?

2. What makes you feel welcomed in another person's home? What do you do to make others feel welcome in your home? How do we practice those things as a community?

3. Who are the "lepers in your head"—the people you would rather not be seated with?

CHAPTER 8: TOTAL AUTHENTICITY

1. Have you ever revealed something about yourself and then regretted it? Have you ever revealed something and found real acceptance and connection? What made the difference?

2. How can your church show newcomers that they are free to be their authentic selves in your community?

3. Does your church expect its pastors to be "on their best behavior" or to share the messier parts of themselves? What impact do you think this has on people?

CHAPTER 9: TRUE DIVERSITY

1. What's the most diverse group you have been a part of? In what ways was it diverse? How does diversity affect the way the group functions?

2. The author says on page 85, "The work of diversity is often left as only a noble aspiration that hopes the desire for inclusive community is itself enough to create it—and usually it isn't." What actions are required to make true diversity a reality?

3. What kinds of conflict can flare up when people are pursuing diversity? How can you work through these conflicts?

CHAPTER 10: AGENDA-FREE COMMUNITY

1. What is your motivation for inviting people to church? How can you discern between a worthy motive and a hidden agenda?

2. How do you define "evangelism"? What should the church's goal be? Is it possible to be truly agenda-free?

3. What communities are you a part of that feel agenda-free? What does that feel like?

CHAPTER 11: SHOW THEM THE OCEAN

1. Where have you seen churches be "all talk and no action" or a simply theoretical or intellectual endeavor?

2. Having read about the four nonnegotiable "legs" of the bigger table in chapters 7–10, what action do you think is most needed to make the bigger table a reality in your faith community?

3. How does the author's description of the diverse, sometimes contentious gathering he facilitated in California make you feel? What would be your hopes for and hesitations about hosting a similar gathering?

CHAPTER 12: BULLIES, BIBLES, AND BULLHORNS

1. How do we inadvertently put principles before people? What would it look like to approach potentially divisive issues while putting people's hearts and stories first?

2. How can we put people before principles without abandoning our convictions? How do we act on our convictions without doing damage to those who disagree?

3. What "boxes" do you tend to put people in? What would it take to learn their stories and not box them in? What might you discover?

CHAPTER 13: PHARISEES, HERESIES, AND LEAST-LOVERS

1. How do you typically think about problems in the world? Do you have a framework for understanding why people suffer from things like natural disasters, cancer, poverty, or addiction?

2. How does this framework determine the way we respond to people in crisis?

3. What troubled individuals or groups do you need to see with new eyes? How might that change the way you perceive them and their struggle?

CHAPTER 14: THE CHURCH WILL BE QUEER

1. In what ways is the church today countercultural? In what ways does it resemble the surrounding culture?

2. What do you think *should* distinguish the church from the world? How are you and your faith community doing at that?

3. The author says on page 140 that the church should be "on the very front lines . . . leading the charge . . . defining the movement of equality and justice, not bringing up the rear and definitely not digging in our heels and fighting against it with all that we have." Do you agree? Are there any boundaries we should not be breaking?

CHAPTER 15: MAMA BEAR HUGS AND MAMA DRAGON FIRE

1. Describe a time when you've seen a display of radical hospitality, authenticity, diversity, or agenda-free community attract new people to be a part of it or to oppose it.

2. Do you ever hesitate to use your voice out of fear of backlash, trolling, or criticism? What are possible positive outcomes?

3. What are some marginalized groups you could ally with to join together at the bigger table?

CHAPTER 16: A PASTOR, A RABBI, AND AN IMAM WALK INTO A BAR

1. What challenges and barriers do you think other religions face to building the bigger table? Which are the same as those Christians face and which are distinct to other faiths?

2. The author says on page 156 that people sometimes ask, "If you're this open to people of other faiths and you don't have an agenda to share the gospel, . . . why are you still calling it a Christian community? What is left that is distinct?" Is this something you wonder? How would you answer those questions?

3. What could you do to increase dialogue and cooperation between faith communities in your area?

CHAPTER 17: FEAR LESS

1. What scares you most about practicing the faith of the bigger table? What do you think God would say in response?

2. The author says on page 164, "Life now is not a test to try and *reach* God, but an opportunity to notice God." Would you describe your faith journey similarly? What words would you use?

3. What would help rid you of "the fear of getting it wrong"?

CHAPTER 18: IS THE TABLE REALLY BIG ENOUGH?

1. What issues do you feel most polarized on—where you stand clearly on a "side" opposed to "the other side"? What would it look like to stand in the middle and bring those sides together? Can you do it without compromising your beliefs?

2. Do you doubt that the table can ever be big enough for people on "the other side" or that they would even want to sit down? What can bring you hope in the face of those concerns?

3. What are your next steps toward building the bigger table?